REMEMBERING CARLISLE

REMEMBERING

CARLISLE

Tales from the Cumberland Valley

JOSEPH DAVID CRESS

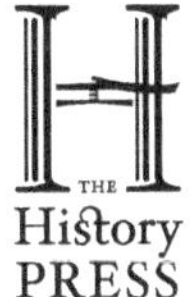

Published by The History Press
Charleston, SC 29403
www.historypress.net

First published 2009

Front cover: Large oil mural of the Carlisle Public Square, circa 1840, painted by Paul Bloser in 1934 for the lobby of the Hotel Argonne in Carlisle. Now part of the museum collection of CCHS; and the Confederate shelling of Carlisle, July 1, 1893, as sketched by Thomas Nast. This scene shows the Confederates shelling the New York Militia in the first block of East High Street. The market house and Bixler building are shown on the right.

Back cover: Cumberland County Court House, on the public square in Carlisle. A postcard made for Cromleigh's Stationery in Carlisle in the 1940s; and lithograph of Molly Pitcher by N. Currier, 1848 (detail).

Manufactured in the United States

ISBN 978.1.59629.777.7

Library of Congress Cataloging-in-Publication Data

Cress, Joseph David.
Remembering Carlisle : tales from the Cumberland Valley / Joseph David Cress.
p. cm.
Includes bibliographical references.
ISBN 978-1-59629-777-7
1. Carlisle (Pa.)--History--Anecdotes. 2. Carlisle (Pa.)--Social life and customs--Anecdotes.
I. Title.
F159.C2C74 2009
974.8'43--dc22
2009040561

Notice: The information in this book is true and complete to the best of our knowledge. It is offered without guarantee on the part of the author or The History Press. The author and The History Press disclaim all liability in connection with the use of this book.

CONTENTS

CONTENTS

ACKNOWLEDGEMENTS

First, I thank my wife, Stacey, for her love, support and understanding through the four intense months of research and writing that went into this manuscript. You are my true inspiration.

Special thanks also go out to friends and family who have encouraged me over the years, including my father, Paul Robert Cress; my best friend, Timothy Wolfe; and longtime supporters, George and Betty Conner.

Next up are all of my past and present editors, including Hannah Cassilly of The History Press. All of you had a hand in helping me shape my skills through challenging demands.

My gratitude also goes out to the hardworking newsroom staff of *The Sentinel*. Through this newspaper, I have perfected my talent to the point that I am able to realize my dream of being an author. I want to thank, in particular, Executive Editor Hope Stephan for her words of encouragement and Chief Photographer Mike Bupp for his help with the cover art.

Lastly, I want to thank the dedicated and helpful staff at the Cumberland County Historical Society, especially photo archivist Richard Tritt, who was instrumental in making both the illustrations and cover art possible.

INTRODUCTION

Welcome to Carlisle history. Sit back, relax and enjoy. This book is for you, the local resident or visitor seeking an overview, a taste of what makes this town in central Pennsylvania so important and distinctive. As you go forth on your journey, be sure to buckle up. There's bound to be turbulence.

From the beginning, Carlisle was at a crossroads. It existed as a rough-and-tumble town on the edge of civilization long before the Wild West. The streets bore witness to riots and jailbreaks, frontier expeditions, an enemy invasion and a parade of champions. There are stories of defiance, protests of injustice, fits of outrage, awkward reunions and the shelling of civilians.

In every case, the challenge for me was what to include in an overview of Carlisle history. There's plenty of material from multiple sources, but I only wanted to touch the reader slightly and highlight the events, people and places that I believe are significant. My goal from the start was to crack open the door for the reader to investigate further and discover a treasure-trove of local history.

I have chosen twenty stories clustered into five time periods starting in 1751 through to the present day. You will notice that many stories mention the square. The intersection of High and Hanover Streets is the heart of Carlisle, an epicenter of local history. Often the scene of turmoil, the square is relatively tranquil these days, carrying on the rich legacy as seat of Cumberland County government.

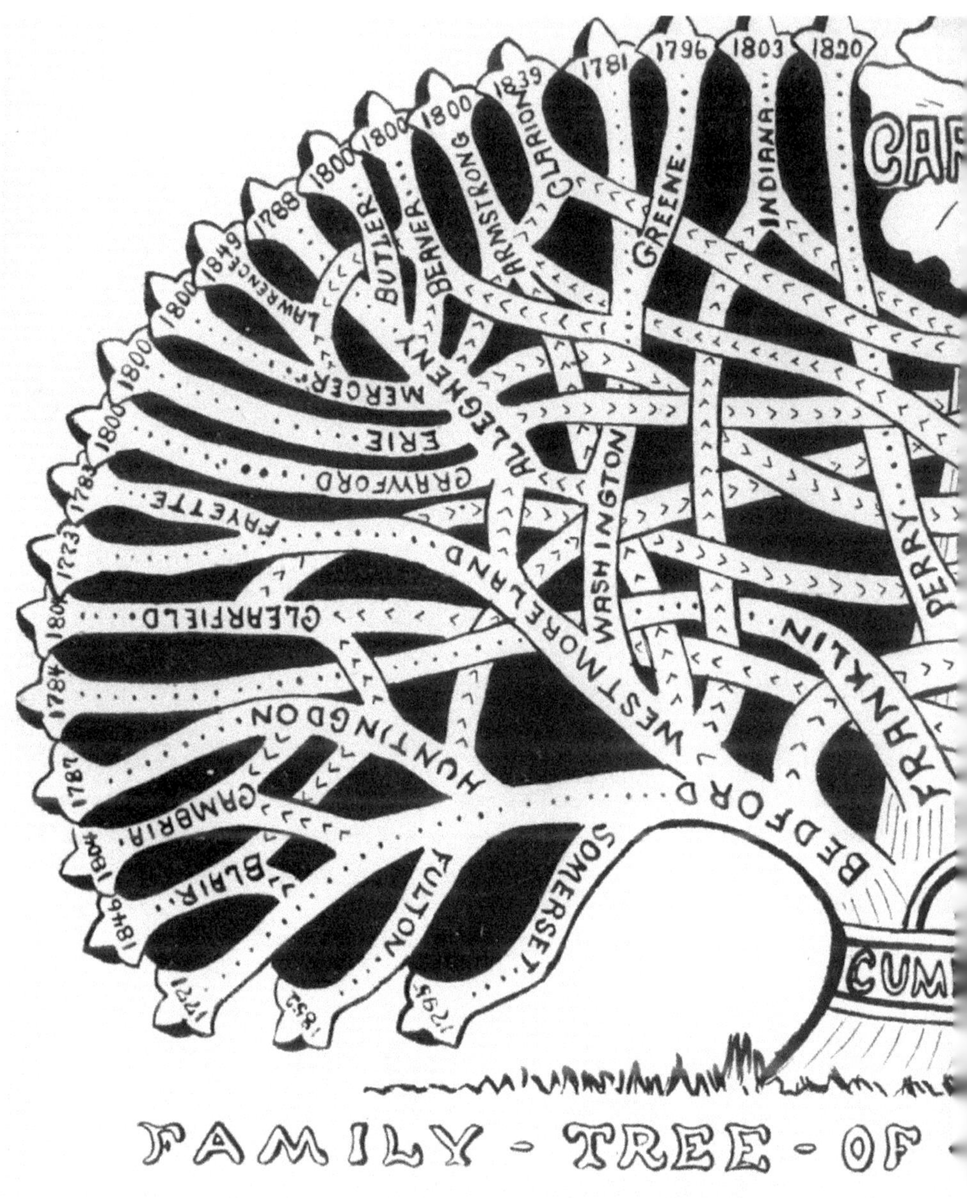

A family tree of Cumberland County designed by Sarah W. Parkinson circa 1909. *Courtesy of CCHS.*

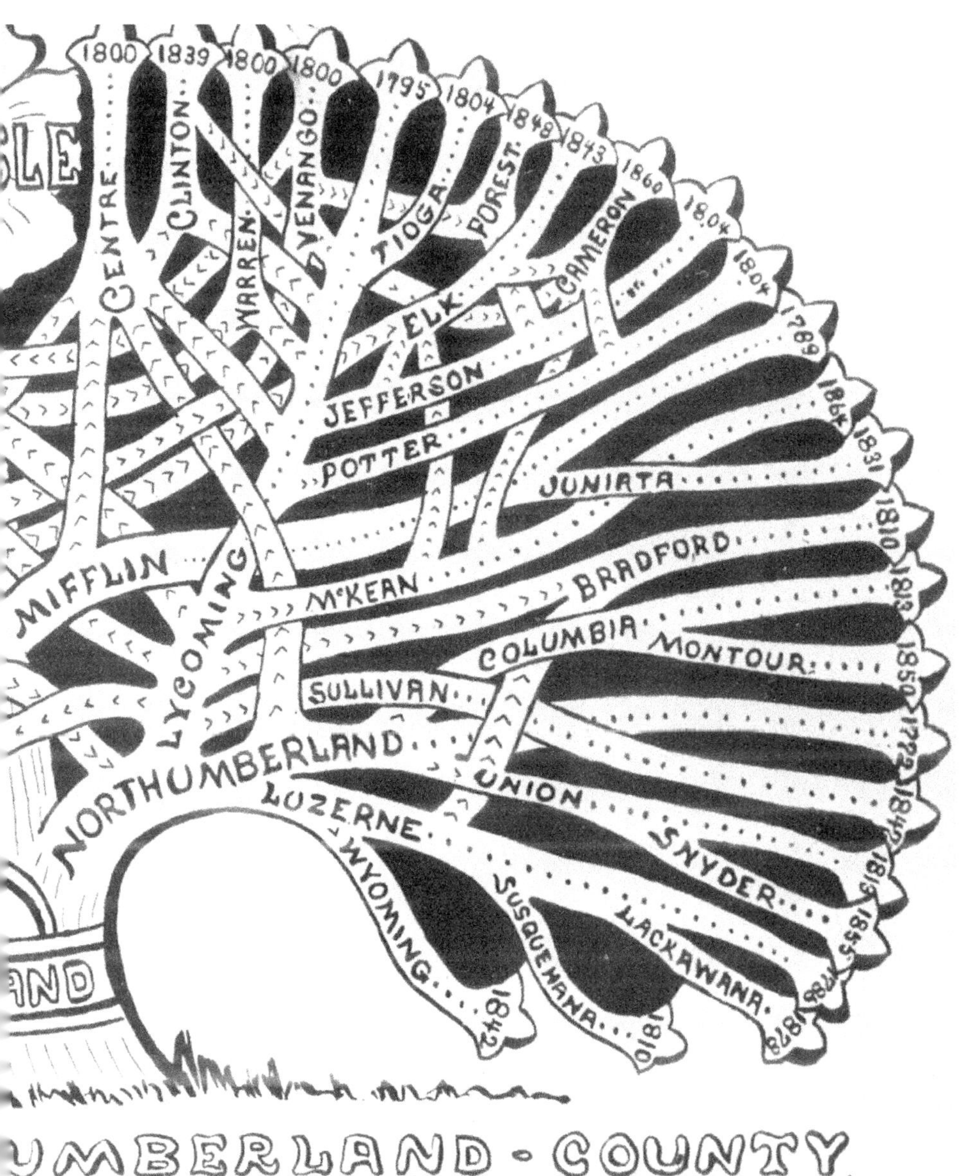
CENTRE
CLINTON
WARREN
VENANGO
TIOGA
FOREST
CAMERON
ELK
JEFFERSON
POTTER
JUNIATA
MIFFLIN
LYCOMING
McKEAN
BRADFORD
COLUMBIA
MONTOUR
SULLIVAN
NORTHUMBERLAND
UNION
LUZERNE
SNYDER
WYOMING
SUSQUEHANA
LACKAWANA
UMBERLAND - COUNTY
Copyright 1909 - S. W. Parkinson

What has changed is the scope of that government. When Carlisle was founded in 1751, the county was much larger, extending from the Susquehanna River west to just beyond present-day Pittsburgh. As time passed, this vast territory splintered into fragments. Forty-eight of the sixty-seven counties of Pennsylvania can trace their territorial roots back to Mother Cumberland.

As for Carlisle, it has always been a strategic transportation hub within the Cumberland Valley, which runs between the Susquehanna River to the east and the Potomac River to the southwest. The town has played a key role in westward expansion and continues to be an important center for logistics, as can be seen by the many warehouses surrounding the borough and by heavy truck traffic on nearby highways.

With transportation comes a military tradition dating from the French and Indian War. Carlisle Barracks is the second oldest military installation in the country and current host of the U.S. Army War College, a premiere school for strategic studies. The Carlisle area is home to thousands of retired military personnel, along with the Army Heritage and Education Center, currently under development. All of this speaks to the influence Carlisle continues to have on the history of Pennsylvania and the United States.

As much as possible, I have used primary sources to tell each story from the participants' point of view. I have found history to be far more engaging when told through the eyes of those who lived it. History was never meant to be drab and dusty but alive and active in its ever-changing impact. It is my hope that readers see within these pages a doorway to open, a window to look through and a pathway to follow to a better understanding.

FAR WEST ADVENTURES

In Cumberland County, the Wild West had an older cousin just as ornery and untamed. As county seat, Carlisle administered land grants for a sparsely populated frontier of mostly Scotch-Irish farmers clustered around churches near streams. Most everyone had to pass through town to do any kind of legal, military or commercial work in the wilderness. The town was born in 1751, about thirty years after James LeTort established a trading post near where Indian paths through the Cumberland Valley intersect. A local creek bears his name. The following sections tell the story of when Carlisle existed as the last major outpost before the savage lands.

"The Rum Ruins Us"

Ben Franklin and the Indian Treaty Talks

The firewater burned with false hope. Reflecting on the scene, Benjamin Franklin saw the seeds of destruction early in his career as a diplomat. It was October 4, 1753, and talks had just ended between tribal leaders of the

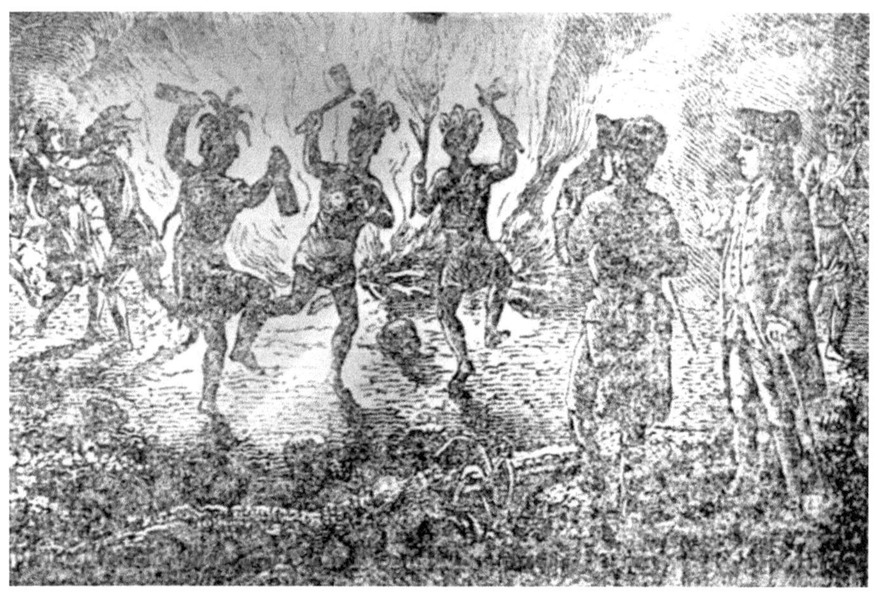

A woodcut of the Indian powwow that followed the treaty conference held in Carlisle. *Courtesy of CCHS.*

Six Nations and a Pennsylvania delegation dispatched to Carlisle by then lieutenant governor James Hamilton.

Together with Richard Peters and Isaac Norris, Franklin had settled in for the night when the three men heard a noise outside their cabin. They investigated, only to find the Indians drunk. Franklin later recalled the experience in his autobiography:

> *Their dark-colored bodies, half naked, seen only by the gloomy light of the bonfire, running after and beating one another with fire-brands, accompanied by their horrid yelling, formed a scene most resembling our ideas of Hell that could well be imagined. There was no appeasing the tumult.*

Just the day before, the Oneida chief Scarouady had spoken against white traders selling rum to Indians, taking advantage of the native tendency toward a lack of moderation. The chief complained that by the time Indians paid the skins to feed their alcohol habits, they were left with nothing to pay off debt on products from fair traders. They would prefer that traders bring valuable goods like gunpowder and ammunition, not flour and rum.

In his book, *A History of the Cumberland Valley in Pennsylvania*, author George Dunehoo recounted the chief's words:

> *The rum ruins us. We beg you prevent its coming in such quantities by regulating the traders. These wicked whiskey sellers, when they have once got the Indians in liquor, make them sell their very clothes from their backs.*

Scarouady had asked the provincial governments of Pennsylvania and Virginia to limit the number of frontier trading posts and to forbid settlement beyond the Allegheny Mountains on lands that had not been purchased from the Indians.

There was fear in Carlisle that September 1753. Settlers from the Allegheny foothills came into town eager to hear the latest news on French forces sweeping down from Canada and into the Ohio Valley. Rumors abounded that the Indians of the west would ally themselves with the invaders amid promises that together they could drive the English back into the Atlantic Ocean.

On September 20, Hamilton received a letter from William Fairfax of Virginia, who had just been in a conference with chiefs of the Six Nations. Tribal leaders wanted to meet with Hamilton in Carlisle on or before September 22 during the return trip to their lands. Hamilton could not go, and the provincial assembly was not in session, so he had to cobble together a delegation from members remaining in Philadelphia.

Hamilton asked Franklin, Peters and Norris to meet with him on September 21. They agreed to use money already appropriated to purchase gifts to present to tribal leaders. As tensions with the French increased over control of North America, it had become vital to enlist as many tribes as possible in favor of neutrality or an alliance with England. The conference in Carlisle would confirm fears that the French had made direct proposals to many tribes, but most had declined involvement. Scarouady and others provided valuable information on the movement of the French and their Indian allies.

On September 22, Franklin and others left Philadelphia on horseback, followed by wagons of goods for the Indians. The delegation arrived in Carlisle on September 26. Running behind schedule, the Indians arrived on the same day. Nearly one hundred men, women and children were lodged in temporary cabins built around a square outside town. The delegates decided early on to forbid the sale of rum to the Indians until after talks were complete. They feared distraction.

"Those people are extremely apt to get drunk and, when so, are very quarrelsome and disorderly," Franklin wrote of the Indians. "When they complained of this restriction, we told them if they would continue sober during the treaty, we would give them plenty of rum when business was over."

Protocol demanded that the delegates first join tribal leaders in paying condolences to Miami and Delaware warriors killed by the French and their Indian allies and to chiefs of the Wyandot tribe who had recently passed away. But to give proper homage, the delegates had to wait several days for the arrival of the wagons and their load of presents. Meanwhile, the delegates, through interpreters, talked with Scarouady and leaders of the Delawares and Shawnees.

They learned that the tribes had twice warned the French not to advance into Indian territory, but to no avail. A tribal council near present-day Pittsburgh resulted in the Indian diplomatic mission to Pennsylvania and Virginia and to envoys being sent to the French to carry a final warning to halt their advance or face war with Indians friendly to the English.

The delegates decided that the gifts on the wagons would not be enough, so they bought more goods in Carlisle. Word came down early on October 1 that the third warning had no effect. The wagons finally arrived before daybreak so the condolence ceremony could start that morning. In attendance were assembly members from Cumberland County, local magistrates and freeholders from the frontier.

History records show that the Indians sat on the floor of the courtroom smoking and testifying their approval or disapproval of the proceedings with grunts. Scarouady was chosen as their prime spokesman and led those gathered in the ceremony. "We wipe your tears from your eyes that you may see the sun, and that everything may become pleasant and clear to your sight, and we desire you would mourn no more," the Oneida chief reportedly told the bereaved. The ceremony continued the following day.

On October 3, Scarouady spoke out against the sale of rum, advocated restraint on westward expansion and called on the English to have only three trading posts selling cheaper goods. The next day, Franklin and his fellow diplomats agreed in principle to three trading posts but advised the Indians that they need to talk to their government. That night, the Indians got drunk on long-withheld rum. Franklin chronicled the turn of events:

> *At about midnight, a number of them came thundering at our door, demanding more rum of which we took no notice. The next day, sensible*

> *they had misbehaved in giving us disturbance, they sent three of their old counselors to make their apology.*

Franklin did not identify who spoke for the Indians, only that the leader acknowledged fault and, in offering up spiritual insight, put the blame on the rum. "The Great Spirit…made everything for some use, and whatever use he designed anything for, that use it should always be put to," Franklin quoted the Indian. "Now, when he made rum, he said 'Let this be for the Indians to get drunk with, and it must be so.'"

"If it be design of providence to extirpate (destroy completely) these savages in order to make room for cultivators of the earth, it seems not improbable that rum may be the appointed means. It has already annihilated all the tribes who formerly inhabited the sea-coast," Franklin wrote following his first real mission as a diplomat. In January 1756, a second Indian treaty conference was held in Carlisle that resulted in a declaration of war against the Delawares, who had joined forces with the French. Franklin did not attend, but Peters and Hamilton were present.

"May Heaven…Assume the Supreme"

The Forbes Expedition

No one suspected blood on the horizon as British forces marched from Philadelphia, confident that they could defeat the French and control the forks of the Ohio. Victory seemed so certain that city dwellers launched their own campaign to raise money for fireworks to celebrate a successful expedition by Major General Edward Braddock. But what followed defeat was years of death and torture perpetrated by the French and their Indian allies on the settlers of western Pennsylvania. Terrorism existed long before 9/11.

Pennsylvania was in the midst of the French and Indian War—the name given to the North American front of a broader global conflict between rival empires. The fighting began in 1754 with a clash between French and British troops in the wilderness of what was then a much larger Cumberland County. British and French colonies existed primarily to further the economies of their mother countries. As such, there was competition for the lucrative fur trade with the native tribes, along with conflict over the westward expansion of British settlers into territory claimed by the French.

When Britain sent fur traders and land surveyors into the Ohio River Valley, France deployed troops to assert its trade monopoly and protect the river as the principal route between French settlements on the Great Lakes and the Mississippi. The stage was set for Colonel George Washington to move in and expel the French from Fort Duquesne, which once guarded the strategic forks at present-day Pittsburgh, where the Allegheny and Monongahela Rivers form the Ohio River. But after a day of fighting, Washington accepted French surrender terms after rain spoiled most of his men's gunpowder, leaving them vulnerable.

This clash helped to spark the Seven Years' War between the French and British empires. The fighting spread beyond North America to Europe, Asia and the West Indies in what Winston Churchill described as "the first world war." In 1755, Braddock marched out of Philadelphia and advanced to within eight miles of Fort Duquesne when his expedition was attacked by nearly seven hundred French and Indian warriors. Retreating in panic, the British force was cut off and destroyed, while Braddock was mortally wounded.

For years, Pennsylvania lacked a militia law because the colonial government was controlled by the Quakers, who are pacifists. They felt no need or desire to create a military because Pennsylvania seemed far away from the French colonies to the north and Spanish colonies to the south. Braddock's defeat left western Pennsylvania defenseless and unprepared to fend off attacks by French and Indian raiding parties, which launched a terror campaign against the isolated farms and settlements of Cumberland County.

Settlers left their farms for the relative safety of Carlisle, and for the first time in fifty years, the reach of westward expansion retreated as refugees clogged the roads heading east. To reverse this, the British prepared a third expedition to Fort Duquesne led by a forty-eight-year-old newly promoted brigadier general named John Forbes, who arrived in Philadelphia in mid-April 1758.

Forbes learned from past defeats. He figured that the Braddock expedition had failed because the force had no place to fall back to and regroup after it was attacked. His strategy was to build a blockhouse every twenty miles

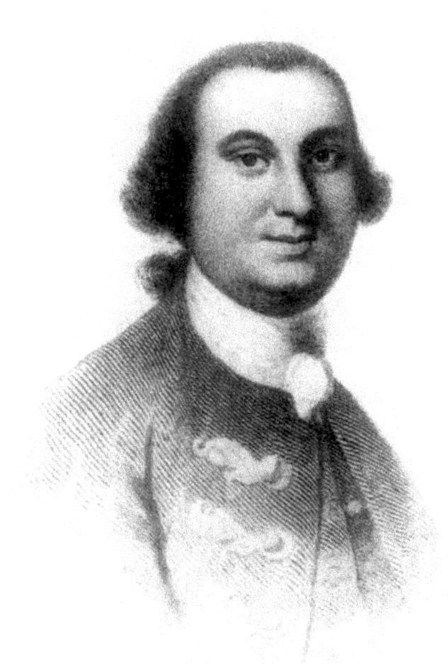
An early engraving of Henry Bouquet. *Courtesy of CCHS.*

and a fort every forty miles to secure his supply line and give his soldiers a refuge if necessary as they advanced on Fort Duquesne. "My offensive operations are clogged with many difficulties owing to the great distance and badness of the roads, through an impenetrable wood, uninhabited for more than 200 miles," Forbes wrote in a letter.

Washington and other Virginia officers criticized this strategy as being too slow. They favored use of the old Braddock Trail. But Colonel Henry Bouquet, along with quartermaster John Burd, sided with Forbes and pushed for the direct route over the mountains from Carlisle west to Fort Duquesne. While an excellent organizer, Forbes was very ill from what historians believe may have been stomach cancer. The sickness made it difficult for him to handle day-to-day management of the expedition, so he delegated that work to Bouquet, a Swiss-born mercenary who served as his second in command.

Forbes argued that his strategy would require more road building but would shorten the march by almost seventy miles and surprise the enemy, who had prepared defenses along the Braddock Trail. Once Forbes decided on a route, he needed an assembly point to launch the expedition. Carlisle was strategically located on the most direct route from Philadelphia to Fort Duquesne. There was already an established road running from Philadelphia through Lancaster and on to Carlisle and Shippensburg.

Carlisle also had a permanent base camp and supply magazine, making it the strongest British position west of the Susquehanna River. This started when early settlers built a stockade and assigned to it a garrison of twelve men. As the first armed force for the community, these men provided the security needed to spur growth in the Cumberland Valley. On March 30, 1757, Colonel John Stanwix arrived in Carlisle with a mixed force of

British and colonial troops. Thus began an association with the military that continues to this day as the historic Carlisle Barracks.

Forbes stayed in Philadelphia for ten weeks to gather troops, supplies and money. On May 11, 1758, Forbes placed an ad in the *Pennsylvania Gazette* seeking wagons for His Majesty's service. Able-bodied men were needed to load and unload supplies bound for Carlisle. Each man was encouraged to bring a gun along for protection. Bouquet was dispatched to Carlisle to coordinate the operation but found only chaos as supplies and troops poured into the rough-and-tumble frontier town. On May 25, 1758, Bouquet wrote to Forbes:

> *I find everything here in utmost confusion. The Provincial troops have no arms fit for service being most of them armed with a heavy musket whose lock is tied with a string. They have not one kettle nor axes or tomahawks.*

As early as March 1758, the streets of Carlisle were packed with soldiers. Many were put up in houses because barracks could not be constructed fast enough to shelter them. Local tradesmen worked hard to keep up on repairs to muskets, wagons, saddles and harnesses. Colonel John Armstrong of Carlisle wrote of the excitement in a March 29, 1758 letter to then deputy governor William Denny:

> *The vigorous efforts determined on by his Majesty through the ensuing campaign must greatly animate every British soul…may Heaven vouchsafe to assume the supreme both by Land & Sea.*

Due to logistical problems, Forbes had to wait until early July to deploy his army from Carlisle. There continued to be problems even after he arrived in town on July 4, as evidenced in a letter written ten days later to Bouquet: "The wagons have been the plague of my life, as I found them here in the greatest confusion."

Forbes stayed in Carlisle for over five weeks to collect and forward supplies to Bouquet, who led the advance west. Illness delayed Forbes from accompanying his army of about two thousand British redcoats and five thousand militiamen, mostly from Pennsylvania and Virginia. When Forbes could be moved, it was by a special cradle suspended between two horses. He pressed on through great agony.

The show of force by the Forbes Expedition prompted the French to abandon and destroy Fort Duquesne, which the British captured without firing a shot on November 24, 1758. It was renamed Fort Pitt and gave the British their first major stronghold west of the Allegheny Mountains. As for Forbes, he returned to Philadelphia, only to die months later from complications due to his illness. Carlisle celebrated the 250th anniversary of the Forbes Expedition in 2008.

"Alone, Yet Not All Alone, Am I"

Indian Captive Regina Hartman

Colonel Henry Bouquet urged the old woman to soldier on past her growing anguish toward a sweet reunion of broken, battered hearts. The Swiss mercenary had seen her distress as she walked in lonesome desperation amidst the communion of strangers gathered in the square in Carlisle.

Magelena Hartman had left her mountain home hoping that she could find her long-lost daughter Regina. Indians had kidnapped her child back in 1755, when Regina was but twelve years old. Now, almost a decade later, hope seemed to fail the old woman, who recognized none of the faces staring back at her. As the story goes, Bouquet felt her pain and came up to the sad woman. "Can't you find your daughter?" he reportedly asked. Struggling with deep inner pain, she could barely manage to say, "No."

"Are you sure? Are there no marks on your child by which you might know her?" he asked.

"None, Colonel. She was a perfect and spotless child," she replied.

Then Bouquet had an inspiration. "Did you never sing to your little girl? And is there no hymn that she was fond of?"

Magelena said there was, so Bouquet suggested that she sing the hymn as they walked along the line of former Indian captives. It was December 31, 1764—a fitting date for a last chance. But the old woman hesitated, telling Bouquet that it was no use. His soldiers would only laugh at her. The colonel insisted, and at last Mrs. Hartman began to sing in a clear but shaky voice the words of an old German hymn: "Alone, yet not all alone, am I."

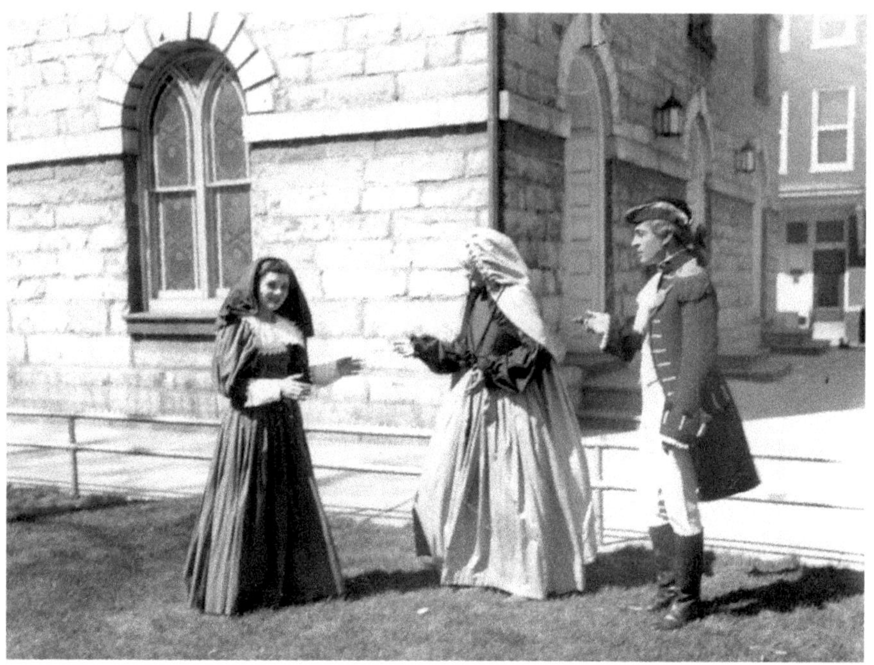

This reenactment of the reunion was held in April 1934 during a pageant celebrating the 200th anniversary of the First Presbyterian Church. *Courtesy of CCHS.*

Everyone turned to witness the touching scene of a woman singing her heart out, her old hands clasped in prayer, her eyes closed, her face upturned in the sun. Then, in the crowd, a shrill voice and a cry for "Mother!" echoed as Regina Hartman rushed to be in the arms of someone she truly loved. Mother and child sang on in joy as two hearts torn asunder were reunited. It had been such a long time coming.

Braddock's defeat in 1755 left the frontier exposed, prompting the French and their Indian allies to launch raids against farms east of the Susquehanna River. One farm belonged to John Hartman, a Lutheran who came to America from Germany and settled in Pennsylvania because of its policies on religious tolerance. Hartman and his wife, Magelena, lived in the Susquehanna Valley near present-day Orwigsburg, Schuylkill County.

There, the couple raised four children—George, Regina, Barbara and Christian. Every night, as they went to bed, Magelena would sing them old German hymns. One morning in October 1755, John Hartman gathered his family for daily devotions. They prayed before having breakfast and making plans for the day.

Mrs. Hartman took Christian, the youngest child, out on a trip to a nearby mill to get flour and to visit a sick friend. John and his fourteen-year-old son, George, went out to finish seeding the last field before the autumn rains. Sisters Regina and Barbara did housework and prepared lunch. All of this serenity was about to be broken.

The record shows that the Hartmans' dog, Wasser, warned his family of danger, but there are slightly different versions detailing the raid on the Hartman homestead. One account had the dog rushing into the cabin. This puzzled the father, who knew that his brave dog would not run from any ordinary enemy. He spoke to the dog, but Wasser stood at the doorway growling with his hackles up. A different version of the story had the family surprised to hear Wasser growl and snarl in the yard. That behavior was unusual for the friendly dog. John Hartman went to the door to investigate. In both versions, Wasser leaped onto an Indian in the front yard, pinning the man to the ground.

There are also different versions of how John and George Hartman were killed. One story had the father running to the door when two gunshots were heard. Both bullets found their mark, killing John outright. George sprang to his father's side but was also struck down. Then the Indians used a tomahawk to kill the dog. A different account had John Hartman going for his gun, but before he could reach it, the door was flung open and several Indians rushed in. They quickly shot the father and son dead before dragging Barbara from the loft, where she was trying to escape.

It is said that Regina threw her hands up to her face and cried, "Herr Jesus, Herr Jesus." In one version, the Indians seized Regina, drew a scalping knife over her lips and told her to keep still. They forced the girls to serve them the leftovers in full view of the two bodies lying across the cabin door. The Indians then tied the sisters together and dragged them out the door. Another girl was tied to a fence post at the edge of the yard crying for her mother. This girl was identified as eight-year-old Susan Smith, whose father, a local farmer, had been killed in an earlier raid. As the children wept, the Indians set fire to the cabin.

Upon her return, Mrs. Hartman could not see the family home and thought at first that she had come the wrong way. She could identify a nearby pine tree but could not see the cabin. Then Christian cried out, "Why mother, where is our house?" Mother and son found only charred ruins. Men from the area tried to pursue the Indians but were poor trackers, and the Indians were moving fast with a head start. However, the men did find the body of Barbara, who had been killed while trying to escape. There was no sign of Regina or Susan Smith.

With Christian by her side, Mrs. Hartman eventually remarried, but time could not ease her grief, and there was no closure while Regina's fate was unknown. Stories speak of a faithful mother who read her Bible every morning and constantly asked God about Regina. In the evening, she would look out into the west and think of her lost love. Her lips would tremble as tears flowed down her wrinkled cheeks. And in those twilight moments, Magelena would sing to herself the old German hymn that would one day reunite mother and daughter: "Alone, yet not all alone, am I."

It is said that Regina was taken to the wilds of western New York, where she lived with an ugly old Indian woman named Shelackla, or "Dark and Rainy Cloud." The old woman would often get drunk on rum and beat both Regina and Susan Smith severely. The girls knew that, if they tried to escape, the Indians would kill them. Besides, they had no idea how to get back home through the wilderness. So they endured the hardship as adopted sisters, speaking to each other in hushed whispers—sometimes in German, but more often in Indian language.

Gradually, they forgot their earlier lives. Regina came to be called Sawquehanna, or "the White Lily," while Susan was Knoloska, or "the short-legged bear." Stories speak of Regina sitting alone for hours, longing for something she could not understand. Deep in her mind were dim memories of a happy home, a kind mother and childhood lullabies but also lingering nightmares of fire, smoke and yelling demons.

Years passed in war and peace before Indian chief Pontiac united the western tribes in a campaign to rid the white man from the frontier. Bouquet marched from Carlisle on August 10, 1764, arriving on September 17 at Fort Pitt, where his army was reinforced by several companies from Virginia. After a brief stop, Bouquet led his men directly into hostile territory. This show of force prompted the Indians to sue for peace on the condition that they release all their white captives into the custody of Bouquet.

Several hundred men, women and children were brought out of the wilderness in a long column, escorted by soldiers who offered protection and rendered aid if the captives had difficulty keeping pace. The column marched for days over rough trails, and history records that the former captives suffered greatly during the cold autumn nights due to their poor clothing. Word was sent ahead informing relatives to meet their loved ones at Fort Pitt, and families came from all over the frontier regions of Pennsylvania, Maryland and Virginia.

Not all of the captives were so eager for a reunion. Many hid in the forest or escaped along the way, refusing to return to their earlier lives. Many were captured in childhood and grew up among the Indians, learning the natives' language and customs. Conway Wing wrote how this altered both the captives' manners and appearance: "The wild mode of life of the Indians, revolting to them at first, had become attractive as old associations became dimmed in their minds."

Other captives had married and found it difficult to part with their Indian families. Susan Smith—fellow captive and friend of Regina Hartman—lost both her parents but was reunited with her aunt and uncle. The remaining captives were escorted to Carlisle, where Regina and her mother found each other.

"Our Chain of Friendship"

The Jailbreak of Murderers

It must have been an easy choice for the poor jailer: keep still and quiet, he would probably live; resist and make noise, he would possibly die. History records how two men entered the common room of the Carlisle Jail and asked for a dram of liquor. It was the morning of January 29, 1768.

When the jailer returned with the drinks, he was surprised to see that other men had entered the jail. Newspaper accounts report how the intruders drew a cutlass and brandished a pistol as they seized and detained the jailer in another room under guard.

Reports vary, but between sixty and eighty armed men entered Carlisle undetected and surrounded the jail. Some believe that the raiders inside used a sledge, crowbar and axe to break open the dungeon door. Others assert that they got the keys from a girl who worked at the jail. No matter, they lit a candle and went down to the dungeon, where Frederick Stump and John Ironcutter lay handcuffed. A jailbreak was in progress.

Local magistrate John Armstrong and county sheriff John Holmes braved the ring of men to enter the jail through the front door. They were pushed back several times by the unruly mob armed with muskets and tomahawks. Armstrong and Holmes were soon joined by Reverend John Steel and

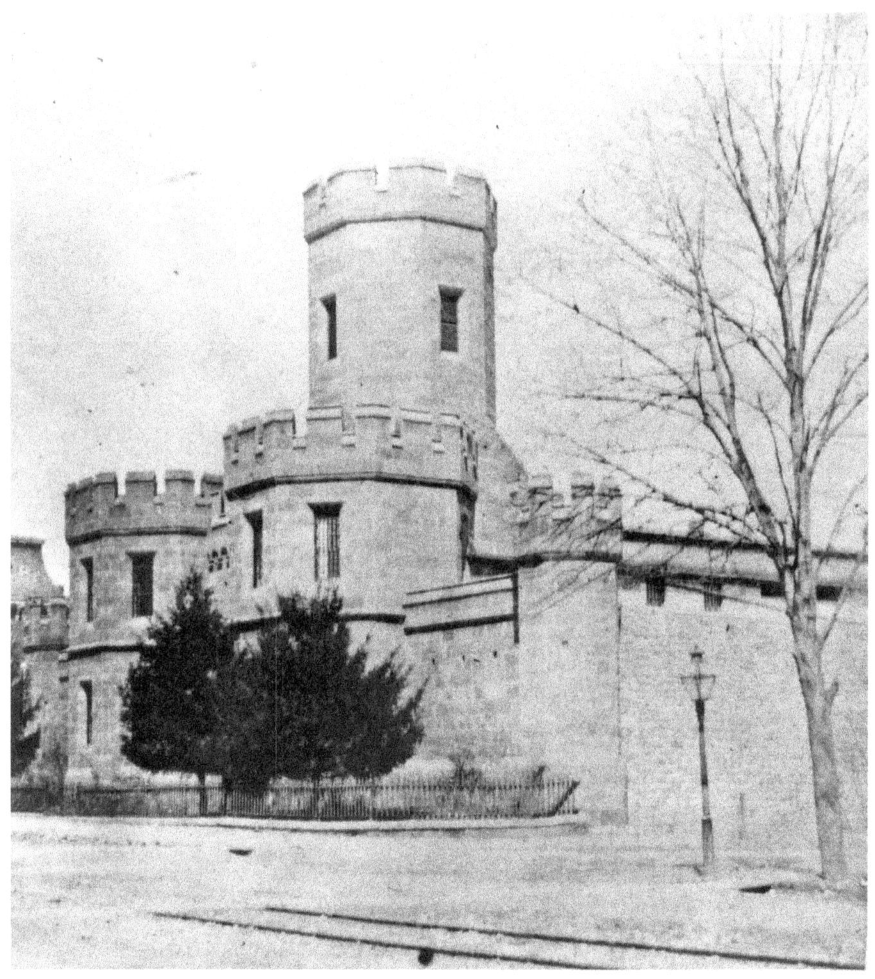

The old jail at High and Bedford Streets was built on the site of the original jail where Stump and Ironcutter were held. *Courtesy of CCHS.*

magistrates Robert Miller and William Lyon. Together, they managed to get to the door, where they vowed to defend the jail with their lives, unaware of what was going on inside.

Meanwhile, the raiders came to the door with the prisoners in tow and forced their way out. When Holmes tried to seize Stump, a raider made a thrust with a cutlass, narrowly missing the sheriff's throat. The jail defenders were soon overpowered and carried off, unhurt, to the middle of the street, where they were held while the prisoners were led away. The mob paused only briefly to force a local smith to remove the shackles from Stump and Ironcutter. The jailbreak took only minutes.

This whole affair had started innocently enough. Several friendly Indians went to a cabin on Middle Creek north of Carlisle to ask its occupants, Stump and Ironcutter, for food or work. Drunk at the time, Stump fought with the Indians, and in the struggle that followed, he and Ironcutter killed four men and two women. The rest escaped. The murderers cut holes in the ice of a nearby creek to conceal the bodies. The next day, Stump and Ironcutter went to a cabin about fourteen miles up the creek and killed an Indian woman and three children. They set fire to the cabin to burn the bodies.

News of the murders spread rapidly. There was concern among settlers that the brutal killings could inflame a native passion for revenge and reignite open conflict on the frontier. Justice demanded swift action by civil authorities to apprehend and prosecute both men in order to preserve the public faith and current treaties with the native tribes. Settlers and Indians had lived together in relative peace since 1764. The brutality of the killings threatened that harmony, along with complaints by tribal leaders of settlers claiming Indian land west of the Allegheny Mountains that had yet to be purchased by the provincial government.

Captain William Patterson lived only twenty miles from Stump. Hearing of the murders, he paid nineteen men two shillings and sixpence per day to help capture the murderers. Before the men could arrive, Stump fled into the woods, but Patterson had a plan. He told some of Stump's friends that the hunting party wanted him to help kill Indians at Great Island. The ruse worked. Someone went out to bring Stump back to a friend's house, where Patterson waited. The murderers were arrested and taken to Carlisle Jail without delay.

After capturing the murderers, Patterson dispatched a messenger to tribes on the west branch of the Susquehanna to express both sorrow and hope for justice. The message stated that Pennsylvanians disapproved of the conduct of the two prisoners, who would no doubt be found guilty and executed. History, of course, had other plans.

"Brothers, I am being truly sensible of the injuries done to you," the message read. "I only add…with our hearts wish…you may not rashly let go to the fast hold of our chain of friendship for the criminal conduct of one of our men." Patterson also called on the Indians to continue their trade with settlers at Fort Augusta near where the murders took place.

Later, the chief justice of Pennsylvania issued a warrant requiring that Stump and Ironcutter be transported to Philadelphia for examination. The high court mandate was a topic of conversation in Carlisle. Residents were of the opinion that the murderers were going to be tried in Philadelphia. Several protested the transport of the prisoners, saying it would create a precedent. Local magistrates resisted the mandate, claiming that jurisdiction in this case rested in Carlisle and the warrant violated the county's right to try criminals in its court.

Other factors played into the decision to keep Stump and Ironcutter in Carlisle until the motives of the authorities in Philadelphia could be determined. Bad weather made passage over the Susquehanna River hazardous, prompting concerns that Stump's friends could attempt a rescue should the sheriff and his party be detained on the West Shore. By then, rumors had spread all over Cumberland and adjacent counties that the prisoners were being ordered to Philadelphia for trial.

There were signs that trouble was brewing. Holmes found a letter from an anonymous source with information that groups had formed in the frontier to rescue the prisoners. All of these factors combined convinced the local magistrates to detain the prisoners in Carlisle instead of complying with the warrant. No one expected a mob to infiltrate the town, seize the jail and release Stump and Ironcutter.

Holmes resisted when the magistrates ordered the sheriff not to proceed with the prisoner transport. The sheriff said he was bound to the authority of the chief justice.

Following the jailbreak, county officials gave chase, overtaking some of the raiders just outside of town. The rest of the raiders escorted the prisoners over the hills into Sherman's Valley, where it is believed the mob had originated. The stragglers promised to return Stump and Ironcutter on the condition that they would not be sent to Philadelphia. There was talk of holding the trial on the frontier, but negotiations broke down after a rumor circulated that the provincial government was ready to send troops to escort the murderers to Philadelphia for trial.

As for Stump and Ironcutter, they escaped into the frontier. It is said that they were never seen nor heard from again by authorities, though efforts were made to hunt them down. The provincial assembly budgeted £3,000 toward the search. On March 16, 1768, Lieutenant Governor John Penn issued a proclamation ordering government and court officials to be diligent in their search and use all possible means to apprehend the fugitives.

Penn believed that Stump and Ironcutter were either hiding out in Pennsylvania or had escaped to a neighboring colony. Again, he emphasized the importance of keeping peace with the Indians as a reason for bringing the murderers to justice. As an incentive, Penn offered cash rewards of £200 and £100 for the capture of Stump and Ironcutter, respectively.

Penn also issued a description of the fugitives at the time of their escape. Stump was thirty-seven years old, about five feet, eight inches tall, a "stout active fellow" and "well proportioned," having black hair with "small black eyes with a downcast look." A native of Lancaster County, Stump was born to German parents and could speak that language well. His English was not as good. He wore a light brown coat, a great coat, an old hat, leather breeches, blue leggings and moccasins.

John Ironcutter was nineteen, about five feet, six inches tall, a "thick clumsy fellow" and "round shouldered," with a dark brown complexion, a smooth, full face, gray eyes and short brown hair. A native of Germany, he spoke very little English. Ironcutter wore a blanket coat, an old felt hat, buckskin breeches, a pair of long trousers, coarse white stockings and shoes with brass buckles.

Since county officials resisted the warrant, the provincial government suspected that they had been part of the plot to free the murderers. In a letter to Lieutenant Governor Penn, the assembly pushed for an immediate investigation of the county officials to determine why they "acted on open contempt of orders" and disobeyed the king's process. Their actions were labeled "rash and insolent."

A review by the provincial council found that the magistrates had interfered with due process when they ordered Holmes not to transport the prisoners. However, the council found no proof of a conspiracy or malicious contempt of the authority of the chief justice. Instead, the council determined that the magistrates had acted in the best interest of the public "in a case of perplexity, not expecting…the consequences which followed." The council advised Armstrong, Miller and Lyon to focus only on matters of county jurisdiction and not to interfere again "in matters which belong to superior authority."

TURN OF THE REVOLUTION

War with France was expensive, prompting the British to reassert sovereign rule over the American colonies and to insist that settlers pay more in taxes to fund the defense of the empire. However, the colonists saw themselves more as equal partners in the victory and felt betrayed by this turn of events. They resisted.

What emerged out of Carlisle and Cumberland County was a frontier spirit of independence, a natural distrust of the Crown and strong leaders capable enough to grasp victory from Revolution. What remains for us is the legacy found in the Old Graveyard on East South Street.

A Trade in Murder

The Trial of James Smith

It could have been the plot of a spaghetti western with a side order of *CSI*. Only this story was true. The popular leader of a band of outlaws was stuck in county jail, locked up in shackles on a trumped-up murder charge. The authorities wanted him to pay for displaying outright defiance in trying to stop illegal arms shipments to Indians raiding settlers on the frontier.

Denied at first due process, our hero was optimistic that justice would be served once the jury heard about the powder burns on the body of his alleged victim. But before he could even go to trial, James Smith had to stop an unruly mob from tearing apart the Cumberland County jail in Carlisle. Settlers never forgot how Smith led his Black Boys in a campaign of rebellion against the Crown some ten years before Lexington and Concord.

Smith grew up on the frontier and, from an early age, was part of its untamed spirit. At eighteen, he was captured by Indians during the failed 1755 expedition by Braddock to seize Fort Duquesne. Smith spent the next five years learning frontier survival skills from the Indians before escaping in July 1759. This experience left Smith with both knowledge of the Indians and strong feelings against the sale of arms and liquor to the natives.

In early 1765, the king issued a proclamation banning trade with the Indians. Settlers supported the measure because of all the friends and family killed by Indians using French and British weapons. Like many others, Smith believed that it was time for the provincial government to end what he called a "trade in murder."

But the traders had other ideas. They had stored goods and invested money in the western trade routes and were supported by eastern merchants out for their own share. Fearing a return of war parties, local residents asked one wagon train to turn back because it carried knives, hatchets, gunpowder and ammunition into Indian territory. But such appeals were met only with insults and outright refusals.

Witnessing this attitude, Smith formed the Black Boys to destroy illegal shipments of Indian trade goods passing through the frontier. He became captain of the group, so named because members blackened their faces prior to going into battle. For this unit, Smith selected the most active young men available, dressed them in native clothing and taught them the Indian tactics of mobility and camouflage.

Westward expansion into Indian land prompted renewed attacks, but this time settlers were determined to stand up against the natives instead of evacuating their homes. What's more, experience taught the settlers not to rely on the Pennsylvania colonial assembly to help fend off the Indians. As a result, settlers began to regard their own laws and magistrates as having greater authority than the Crown for resolving conflict.

In such an environment, the Black Boys became a source of security for Cumberland Valley residents. When the men ambushed a pack train and set fire to the goods, Indian tradesman Robert Callender complained of the attack, saying that it had destroyed the king's property.

Later, the British captured a group of Black Boys and held them at Fort Loudon in present-day Fulton County. Friends and neighbors feared that the British commander would send the prisoners to Carlisle Jail, where they would lose the right to a trial by a jury of their peers. But Smith had other ideas. He raised an army of over three hundred riflemen, who, on March 9, 1765, marched on Fort Loudon and demanded the release of the prisoners.

Each time the British commander sent out runners from the fort, the Black Boys captured them. Soon, Smith had twice as many prisoners as the British. Talks followed, leading to the release of the captives from the guardhouse. However, the British violated the terms of the truce and withheld the frontiersmen's rifles. On May 28, 1765, Smith and four Black Boys captured the British commander and threatened to take him farther into the wilderness if he did not return the rifles. The officer caved to Smith's demands.

Later, the garrison at Fort Bedford captured settlers posing as Black Boys who raided a pack train of Indian goods. Smith thought that the men should be tried by civilian authorities, not the military. With that in mind, Smith called on former Black Boys to join him in a surprise attack to not only capture Fort Bedford but also to release its prisoners. The success of this mission embarrassed British forces in North America and made Smith a marked man overnight.

A week went by without any reaction to the attack on Fort Bedford, so Smith thought it was safe for him to travel in the area again. He set out with three other men—this time to survey land west of Fort Ligonier, only to be betrayed by rumors of an impending Black Boys raid on another wagon train. After receiving a tip from an informant, Callender sent four armed men into the wilderness around Bedford in search of Smith. The men caught up with Smith about five miles west of Fort Bedford. As they surrounded him, one of them reportedly called out, "Surrender; or you are a dead man."

Caught by surprise, Smith thought that they were thieves. They whipped out their pistols and leveled them at Smith. In the struggle that followed, one man snapped a pistol at Smith, who misfired his gun. A fatal bullet struck down one of Smith's traveling companions. Before Smith could reload, the four men overpowered and arrested him for the murder of his fellow traveler, despite pleas by Smith that his gun had misfired. Smith was taken to Fort Bedford and confined to its guardhouse pending further court action.

A trial was held quickly before a handpicked jury, which included friends of the traders. Smith was found guilty of murder and secretly transferred to

Carlisle Jail to prevent a rescue attempt by settlers friendly to his cause. This strategy didn't work. The people found him anyway. Reports vary, but as many as six hundred friends and neighbors of James Smith rallied together in a protest march on Carlisle to demand his release. Many were Black Boys or residents from Bedford, Smithton and the surrounding area.

A delegation of local residents met with the group outside Carlisle, urging them not to make a bad situation worse. They feared the spilling of innocent blood. The Black Boys agreed to send a messenger to talk to Smith and bring back a letter from him verifying his desire to stand trial. Confident of being acquitted, Smith wrote the letter, but the messenger noticed that he was still in shackles and passed on that information to the Black Boys. Angry, they resumed their advance on Carlisle, bent on tearing down the jail if necessary to free their leader.

Hearing this, Smith asked the jailor to remove the irons so that he could thrust his arms out the window as proof his hands were free. The leg irons were also removed. Appearing at his cell window, Smith tried to assure the crowd that justice would prevail, but he must stay in jail and stand trial to be properly exonerated. Smith thanked the crowd for its support before asking his supporters to leave in peace. The crowd started home, but was met along the way by several hundred other people coming to participate in the rescue. Some rioters were settlers from as far away as the Potomac River. In the end, they were persuaded to heed Smith's advice and return home.

Smith stayed in jail for four months, until the case went to trial in January. Friends of Smith asked Cumberland County coroner William Denny to assemble a more objective jury to take to Bedford. There, the body was exhumed, and the investigators examined the victim's clothing. Powder burns found around the bullet hole indicated that the shot had come from extremely close range, yet witness testimony established that Smith had been twenty-three feet away from the victim.

When investigators test-fired the gun from that range, they found that the bullet holes showed no powder burns. This proved that the fatal shot could not have been from Smith's gun. Instead, the evidence suggested that one of the four men who arrested Smith had fired the fatal shot from very close range. Despite this finding, Smith was never granted bail in Carlisle. Throughout the trial, Smith thought that the judges were unfair because they consistently ruled against the admission of defense testimony.

But local justice William Smith managed to have Denny's inquest results entered before the jury. In arguing the case, William Smith also stressed how the arresting party never searched his client's luggage, which proved he had been on a harmless trip. The jury found James Smith not guilty. One judge was so angered by the verdict that he scolded the jurors, saying that none would ever be appointed to public office in Cumberland County.

Freeholders...Freemen

Voices Against Tyranny

William Lyon only had to walk to the north side of the square to show where he stood on the question of independence. It is said that a large crowd gathered in Carlisle in mid-June 1776 to debate the merits of separation from the mother country. A local attorney, his name lost to history, argued that a split was nothing but sheer folly and madness given the vast wealth and military power of the British Empire. He felt that the only option for the weak and impoverished colonies was to sue for peace and seek another way to redress grievances. To do otherwise would invite disaster.

Lyon came forward to argue in favor of independence. His precise words are unknown, but his request has been passed down through generations. He asked those who favored separation to walk to the north side of the square and those against to move to the south side. History records that a great majority picked the north, none went south and only three or four indecisive souls lingered at the center of the crossroads. There is no mention how the skeptical attorney cast his vote, but for Lyon, there could be no doubt on the question of loyalty. His was not the only voice against tyranny to be heard from Carlisle.

Two years prior, "freeholders" and "freemen" had held a meeting on July 12, 1774, at the First Presbyterian Church on the square. Church elder John Montgomery presided. The meeting was called after Parliament passed the Coercive or Intolerable Acts, which closed the port of Boston in retaliation for the Tea Party.

Men from across Cumberland County passed resolutions condemning the British for subverting the rights and liberties of not only Boston and Massachusetts residents but also those living in all the colonies. The suffering

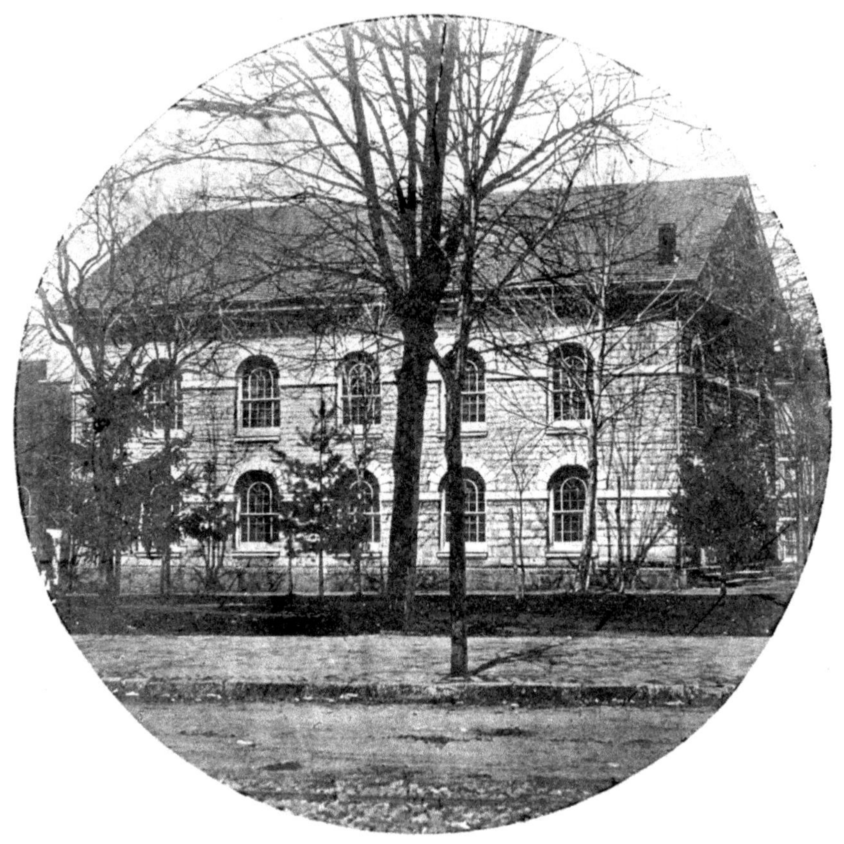

The earliest known photo of the First Presbyterian Church, taken by Charles Lochman circa 1865. *Courtesy of CCHS.*

of Boston became a common cause. The belief among many Pennsylvanians was that if one port could be closed, other seaboard cities could be shut down, including Philadelphia. This would jeopardize inland commerce and cause the whole economy to suffer.

The resolutions also called for an agreement not to import goods from Britain and to send aid to Boston if deemed necessary. There was also support for the formation of a Congress of Deputies to vigorously pursue a redress of grievances against the king and Parliament. Three members of the First Presbyterian Church—James Wilson, Robert Magaw and William Irvine—were appointed to represent Cumberland County in an assembly of delegates from all counties in Pennsylvania. Magaw would later serve as a colonel in the Continental army, while Irvine, a physician by trade, was a Revolutionary War general.

In 1774, Wilson gained widespread recognition as author of a forty-five-page pamphlet arguing that Parliament had no authority of any kind over the colonies. Wilson declared that all men, by nature, are free and equal. This made him one of the earliest advocates for independence. Wilson would later cast the deciding vote in Pennsylvania's decision to separate from England.

Wilson was also one of three men, with ties to Carlisle, who signed the Declaration of Independence. The other men were George Ross and James Smith—two out-of-town attorneys who practiced law in Cumberland County. Himself a lawyer, Wilson lived in Carlisle until 1777 and then moved to Philadelphia. He later served on the convention that framed the U.S. Constitution and was appointed by President George Washington to the U.S. Supreme Court.

As for Lyon, he first came to the Cumberland Valley in 1750 as an assistant to his uncle, Colonel John Armstrong, an elder of the First Presbyterian Church. Lyon worked as a surveyor, a justice of the peace, a military officer and a court official. As an early advocate for independence, Lyon represented Cumberland County on the Council for Safety, which was responsible for military operations in Pennsylvania.

On October 6, 1776, Lyon proposed the formation of a militia called "the flying camp" to protect the colony from incursions in the frontier by British forces, Tories and Indians. The name "flying camp" came from the soldiers being on call for quick action in the event of emergency. Two other men with ties to the church also played major roles in the Revolution. Ephraim Blaine entered the army as a colonel to become its commissary general, while William Thompson is said to have been the first colonel commissioned in the U.S. Army.

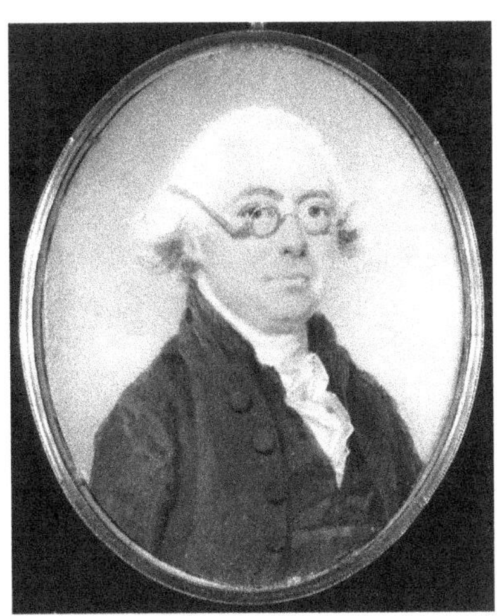

A portrait of James Wilson by Jean Elouis. *Courtesy of CCHS.*

During the war, Congress established Washingtonburg—the first place named after the future president. Carlisle was selected because of its strategic location, quality road network and the availability of buildings erected by the former British garrison. Complete with forges and workshops, Washingtonburg was an important logistics center providing munitions and supplies to the Continental army. Its facilities included an artillery school and hospital. German prisoners of war constructed the Hessian powder magazine that stands today at Carlisle Barracks.

"Submitted to Alarms and Jealousies"

John Andre and the Tories

There was no doubt in John Andre's mind—the boy had talent beyond just a ticket home. Writing from Carlisle, the captured British officer tried to assure Caleb Cole of his son's natural ability in painting. "He is greatly improved since I left Lancaster and I do not doubt if he continues his application, he will make very good progress."

There was a time in early April 1776 when Andre had encouraged Cole to send his son to Carlisle so that the boy, his star pupil, could benefit from more lessons. Andre wrote:

> *My desire was to find a lodging where I could have him with me, and some quiet honest family of friends or others where he might have boarded, as it would not have been so proper for him to live with a mess of officers.*

The young lieutenant pressed the father, hoping that he would consent to have his son be an apprentice. Andre figured that it might be the excuse he needed to quit the army, resign his commission and return to England. The father would not budge, and Andre was unsuccessful in finding a place in Carlisle for the boy to live. "I…am myself still in a tavern," Andre wrote. Later, when his welcome turned sour, Andre could forgive Cole for not sending his son to Carlisle. Still, he had sage advice for the father to teach his child the fine art of patience:

> *I cannot regret that you did not send your son hither. We have been submitted to alarms and jealousies which would have rendered his stay here very*

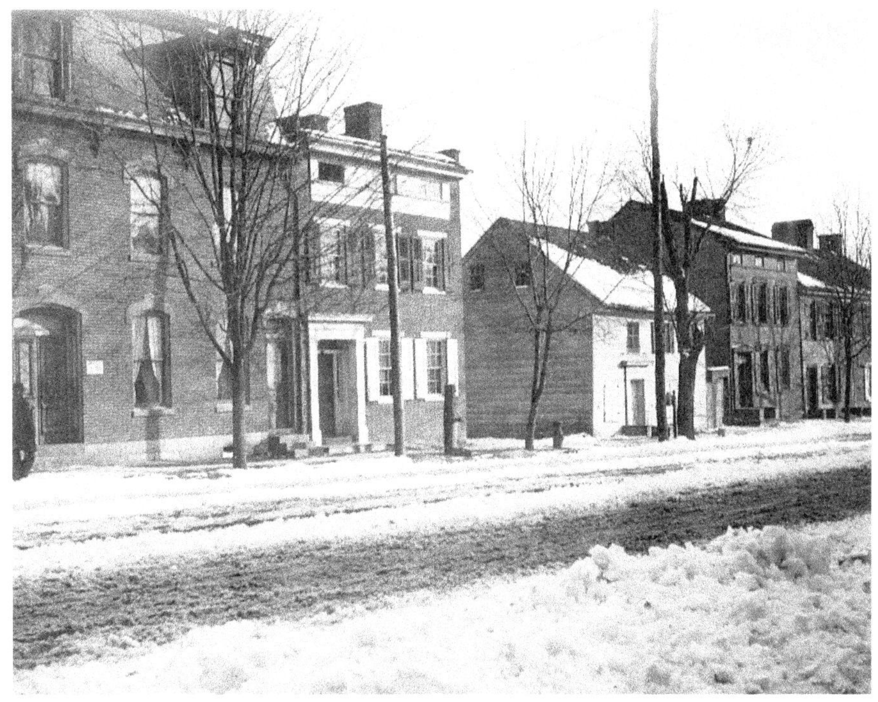

The brick house is on the site of the house where Andre was confined. The weatherboard house belonged to Mrs. Ramsey. *Courtesy of CCHS.*

> *disagreeable...I would not willingly see any person suffer on our account... Let him go on copying whatever good models he can meet with...With a little practice, this will be natural to him, that his eye will at first sight guide his pencil in the exact distribution of every part of the work.*

Andre was described as a graceful, dashing young officer with a serious but somewhat tender expression on his face. Born in England of French descent, Andre was the son of a merchant. He was educated in England and Switzerland and was proficient in French, German and Italian. Andre was also very accomplished in music, drawing and verse.

At twenty, Andre left a job at a countinghouse to join the British army. He was captured at Saint John during the failed attempt by the American army to invade Canada in the fall of 1775. Prisoners taken in the campaign were quickly moved to the interior to prevent their escape. First confined in Lancaster, Andre was later sent to Carlisle, arriving there in April 1776. He was with a group of British officers that included Lieutenant John Despard.

The common practice was to find room for prisoners in private homes, but Andre complained about how Carlisle residents were unwilling to harbor them. Andre and Despard also had trouble securing money for expenses from the British government. Quarters were arranged in a small stone tavern located on the northeast corner of South Hanover Street and Chapel Alley. A Mrs. Ramsey lived across the alley and would occasionally speak to the men or send them a loaf of bread.

Due to their rank, Andre and Despard were afforded privileges beyond the ordinary soldier and were allowed to hunt game no farther than six miles from Carlisle. They were required to wear their uniforms when outside town boundaries. One day, Mrs. Ramsay saw Andre and Despard converse with two suspected Tories. She reported this immediately to the Committee of Public Safety. The Tories fled but were caught by local residents, who confined all four men to county jail while authorities investigated.

The Tories had in their possession letters written in French, but no one could translate the text. It was assumed that the letters were messages meant for the British officers. With their privileges revoked, Andre and Despard could not leave the tavern out of uniform and not at all after dark. Unable to hunt, they destroyed their guns in protest, saying, "No damned rebel would ever burn powder in them."

Tempers flared as the Revolution gathered momentum, making it more dangerous for Andre and Despard to walk Carlisle streets. It is said that they were sometimes pelted with stones, garbage and curses. Andre wrote how one resident brandished a hatchet to remind him of "its agreeable effect on the skull."

This tension reached a climax when a group of young men led by a Captain Thompson came over Sterrett's Gap, marched into Carlisle and stopped in front of the tavern. History records that the men were upset that American prisoners held by the British were dying from starvation while Andre and Despard lived in relative comfort. It was believed that Andre had showed indifference to colonists being mutilated and mistreated in Canada.

They wanted to lynch the British officers but were stopped by Mrs. Ramsey, who recognized Thompson as a former apprentice to her husband. She persuaded him not to violate the prisoners' rights. As they left, Thompson shouted back, "You can thank my old mistress for your lives." Grateful, Andre and Despard sent Mrs. Ramsey a box of high-quality candles, but she returned the gift, saying that she was too much of a Patriot to accept a gratuity from them.

Later, Andre wrote how Carlisle is inhabited by a

> *stubborn, illiterate crew called the Scotch-Irish, sticklers for the Covenant, and utter enemies to the abomination of curled hair, regal government, minced pies and other heathen vanities. A greasy committee of worsted-stocking knaves.*

No longer safe, Andre confined himself to his room and read constantly, his feet propped up on the window sill and his dogs by his side. Eventually, Andre was transferred out of Carlisle as part of a prisoner exchange.

Andre was in Philadelphia when the British occupied the city and was, at one point, a suitor of Peggy Shippen, whose family founded Shippensburg. Instead of marrying Andre, she became Benedict Arnold's second wife. It was Arnold and Andre who conspired to leak sensitive information on the defenses of West Point to Henry Clinton, the British commander in New York City. Andre was stopped by militia on his way to New York and was caught with the incriminating paperwork.

He later confessed to being part of a conspiracy to attack West Point and was sentenced to death by hanging. Washington did not respond to an appeal by Andre to change the punishment to the more traditional execution by firing squad. Andre died on October 2, 1780. News of his death reached Carlisle the following week. It is said that some mourned the young British officer who had hunted small game in nearby fields and forests and waterfowl along the Yellow Breeches and Conodoguinet Creeks.

In October 1776, Carlisle was designated a place of confinement for Tories fighting against the American cause. It is said that secret agents with the British army visited places where war prisoners were confined to contact parolees. Other British agents worked the western frontier, spreading rumors that the Revolution was doomed. They offered settlers large land grants if they joined the British cause.

One group came as far as the Cumberland Valley to plan an invasion and to communicate arrangements with war prisoners held at Carlisle. This band of Tories was ambushed by Indian raiders near present-day Huntingdon, and their leader, John Weston, was killed. Many fled into the wilderness and were arrested later, including John's brother. Thomas Weston was brought into Carlisle but escaped before his trial for high treason. Though he confessed to participation in the plot, he claimed that he had been misled by his brother.

As early as January 1777, John Armstrong wrote to the Council on Safety about the threat of an invasion by Tory forces into the Cumberland Valley.

He reported how proclamations were in circulation to persuade colonists to form such an army should the British invade the valley.

That same year, word came of plans by Loyalists to raise forces to occupy Lancaster and York Counties. There were reports of one hundred Tories available to take Carlisle. There were arrests, but nothing ever developed beyond hurting the morale of the Patriots.

Several Tories left the Cumberland Valley to join British forces in Philadelphia. Colonial authorities responded by seizing their property and putting those who returned in Carlisle Jail. Property was restored to Tories who pledged allegiance to the cause, while the holdings of those who refused were sold.

"THE DEADLY ROAR OF CANNON WITH THE LOW, SWEET VOICE"

Molly Pitcher

As a boy, Wesley Miles was not overly fond of the nurse who cared for his ailing mother. He thought that Molly McCauley was too strict a disciplinarian and too quick for naughty children. "Fleet as a deer, she was sure to catch her object of pursuit in every attempt to escape," Miles wrote to the *Carlisle Herald* in 1876.

As a teacher, Miles recalled the childhood fear of being carried away on her shoulders. Yet, he also felt compelled to write a letter in memory of what he believed was a forgotten legend—a woman history has named Molly Pitcher. "During this Centennial year, something ought to be done about marking the grave of this brave American woman," Miles wrote in his push for recognition.

As a result, a citizens committee was formed that year to raise money for a marble headstone unveiled at Molly's grave site as part of the local Independence Day celebration. It didn't end there. The legend grew that Molly McCauley of Carlisle was the Molly Pitcher of lore and was thus well deserving of upgraded memorials, first in 1905 and then in 1915.

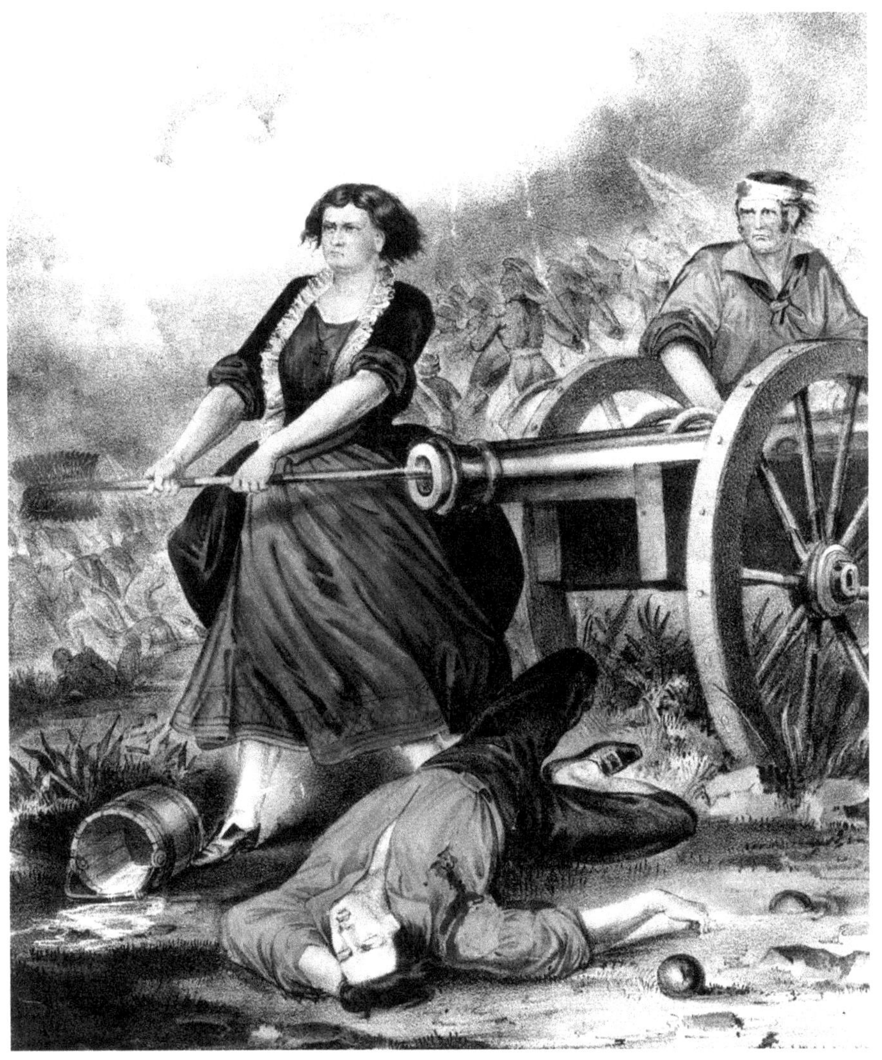

A lithograph of Molly Pitcher at Monmouth by N. Currier, circa 1848. *Courtesy of CCHS.*

A hotel on South Hanover Street is named for the Revolutionary War heroine, along with a civic award presented each year. Anyone can see Molly, larger than life, in the Old Graveyard on East South Street and in a large mural on the side of a building near the northeast corner of North Pitt and West High Streets. Her story is one of struggle to sort fact from folklore, causing some to wonder if the woman buried in Carlisle is the real McCoy or just a misidentified soul. Perhaps the truth is somewhere in between.

Legend has it that Molly Pitcher was a camp follower who accompanied her sweetheart to the Battle of Monmouth on June 22, 1778. Amid the fighting, she carried water to refresh thirsty soldiers suffering in the oppressive heat. When she saw her lover killed or wounded by enemy fire, she promptly took his place at the cannon and helped to load the weapon as soldiers held the line. It is said that George Washington honored her bravery with an official rank.

The trouble is, the record is unclear as to the true identity of Molly Pitcher or even if this episode took place. The Cumberland County Historical Society published a journal article disputing the myth. In it, local historians D.W. Thompson and Merri Lou Schaumann wrote that there is no record of any woman manning artillery at Monmouth.

The first printed reference to the alleged event appeared in 1840 in the published journal of Albigence Waldo, a Connecticut physician who served with American troops. In it, Waldo wrote: "Her gallant, being shot down, she immediately took up his gun and like a Spartan heroine fought with bravery, discharging the piece with regularity."

Waldo wrote how he got the story secondhand from a wounded officer who claimed to have been a witness "and assured me I might depend on the truth."

Thompson and Schaumann believe that, over the years, the story of Molly Pitcher became such an accepted part of Revolutionary War history that no one disputed the 1876 claim that Molly McCauley was the legend. In their paper, they explained how Americans of the nineteenth century tended to believe, without criticism, the popular view of history. Writers of that time sought to discover new anecdotes rather than verify stories.

So when the assertion was made, Carlisle residents bought into it and expressed their support of a headstone for the unmarked grave of Molly McCauley, a Revolutionary War camp follower who died in 1832. The legend grew to the point that an effort was launched in 1905 to lobby state lawmakers to budget $5,000 toward the installation of a cannon and a flagpole at her grave site.

Jeremiah Zeamer, editor of the *American Volunteer* newspaper, sought to debunk the legend but was largely ignored. He felt that her grave was already appropriately marked. "Considering the small and doubtful service Molly McCauley tendered the country, this is about all the respect that can be awarded her memory in justice to history," Zeamer wrote in an April 4, 1905 editorial. "She is neither an historical or moral character to hold up to young Americans for emulation."

In arguing that the legend had been elevated beyond any actual deed, Zeamer wrote that there was nothing in the historical record to authenticate the claim that McCauley had manned the gun. While local residents had heard of McCauley being in the Revolution, no one had heard stories from her about helping to load a cannon. "Had anything so remarkable occurred," Zeamer wrote, "she certainly would have felt sufficient pride in it to remember and sometimes speak of it."

He added that there had been no mention of the alleged incident in obituaries published in two Carlisle newspapers at the time of her death when any story would have been relatively fresh and easy to corroborate. The CCHS article made the same point: "The editors of both papers had long resided in Carlisle, had long known Molly, and presumably would have been glad to have that incident to her credit had she possessed any claim for such a distinction."

But in 1905, a local congressman offered a different spin on Molly when he gave a speech at the ceremony to dedicate the monument. He praised the story of courage under fire as a lasting tribute to the inner strength of women:

> *Her act aroused, almost to a frenzy, the enthusiasm of those about her and held the wavering soldiery in line...The glorious achievements of the man behind the gun are often told, but the woman behind the gun is exceptional and unique. The glories and successes of the gentler sex are not usually achieved by the aid of gunpowder. We do not commonly associate the deadly roar of the cannon with the low, sweet voice.*

A decade later, local residents led the charge to have a monument and statue of Molly Pitcher erected at the site. So who was the Molly of Carlisle fame?

Thompson and Schaumann place her birth at sometime between 1750 and 1755. They say she married William Hays and followed him to the war when he enlisted as a gunner in Proctor's Artillery on May 10, 1777. After the war, in 1783, the couple settled in Carlisle, where Hays operated a barbershop. After Hays died, Molly married John McCalla, only to become a widow a second time. She then married John McCauley in 1813. By the time she died in 1832, she also went by the name of Molly McKolly.

In their paper, Thompson and Schaumann wrote that the Molly of Carlisle fame may have carried water or performed any of the tasks related to being a camp follower. There is simply a lack of evidence to verify that.

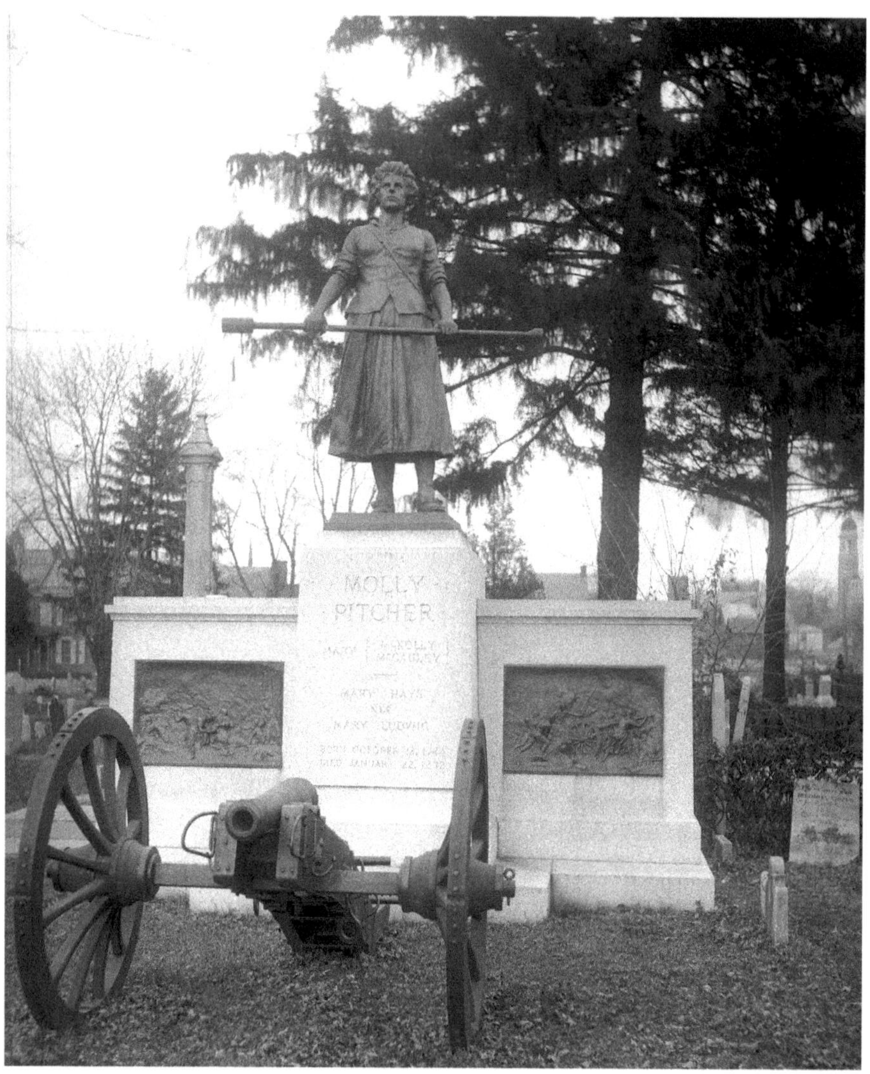

The Molly Pitcher monument, circa 1920. *Courtesy of CCHS.*

They believe that the Molly of Carlisle may have been mistaken for heroine Margaret Corbin.

There is proof that the Molly of Carlisle may have done something distinctive during the war. In 1822, she applied for a pension from the state and was approved that February for an annuity of forty dollars. When the state House passed the bill, the language was amended to show that the annuity was granted because of her service during the war, not because her husband had been a soldier. The records show her receiving the annuity for ten years, sometimes under the name of McKolly, sometimes McCauley.

The *American Volunteer* published her obituary on January 26, 1832. It read that McCauley had lived during the American Revolution, "witnessed many a scene of Blood and Carnage" and was an efficient aid to the sick and wounded. The obituary mentioned no details.

In various newspaper accounts, local residents describe the Molly of Carlisle as a strong, heavyset woman who was very talkative. Though employed sometimes as a nurse, she was hired often to do such menial work as cleaning, scrubbing and washing. Elizabeth de Huff, who lived across the street, said that Molly's coarse appearance was nothing like her personality: "There was something good in her...she was as kind-hearted a woman as ever lived. The roughness was on the outside...she was always willing to sit up at night with the sick."

But not everyone saw Molly in a positive light. In his 1905 editorial, Zeamer described Molly as a "vulgar, profane old woman, uncouth in appearance and notoriously fond of grog." Zeamer felt that bestowing any honor on Molly would send the wrong message to young women:

> *They may ask "Why be good, if goodness is not appreciated. Let us swear, be obscene, get drunk and raise old Ned; for...after we are gone, people* [may] *become possessed of the absurd notion that we helped to fire a cannon."*

Zeamer questioned why Carlisle residents were so eager to honor Molly McCauley with expensive monuments while ignoring such Revolutionary War figures as Generals John Armstrong, William Thompson and William Irvine, who are also buried in the Old Graveyard.

GROWING PAINS

With freedom won, a new country emerged from the Revolution struggling to define itself. Carlisle was again at a crossroads—a scene of violent protests and open defiance to established laws and conventions. The sections that follow show that the frontier town had gumption in taking on the Constitution, a tax on whiskey, a devastating fire and the issue of slavery. As Carlisle grew in population, Cumberland County shrank in territory, and the square was visited by the original commander in chief, officials burned in effigy, a slick arsonist and an abolitionist professor on trial for inciting a riot.

"Lover of Good Order...Lament the Wound"

The Constitution Clash

Chief Justice Thomas McKean was exceptionally well dressed for a dummy. The effigy sported a good-quality coat, hat and wig, along with a ruffled shirt.

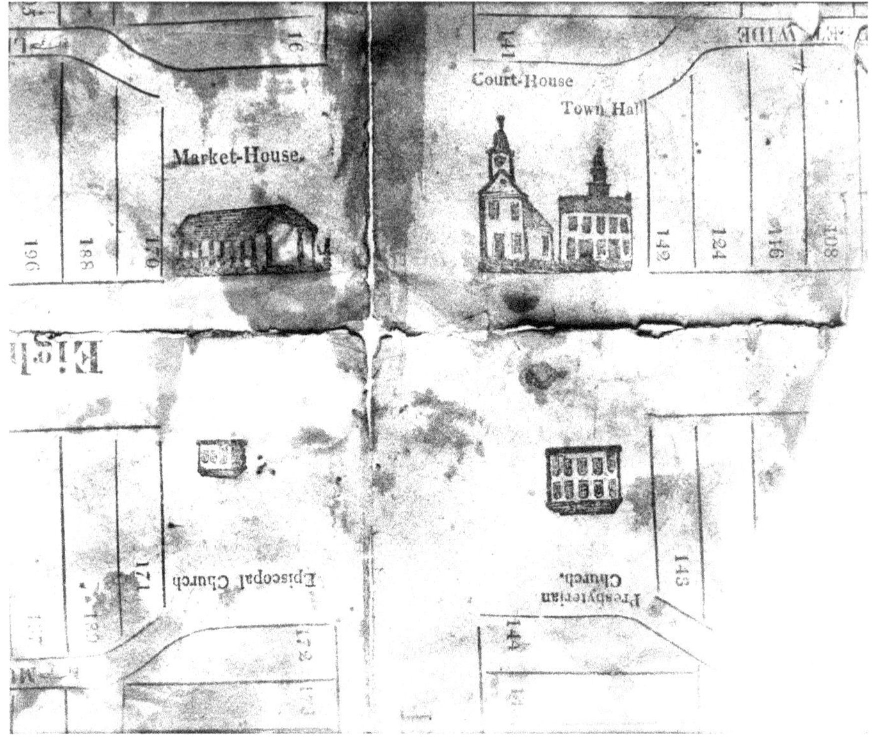

Detail of a map of the square made about 1823 by Holcomb and Tizzard. *Courtesy of CCHS.*

It was reported how Antifederalists paraded likenesses of McKean and James Wilson, a leading supporter of the new Constitution, up and down the streets of Carlisle. Led by Captain Joseph Frazier, the men marched in formation as others gathered more wood for the bonfire on the square. When the time was right, McKean and Wilson were cast into the flames in protest of the recent passage of the federal Constitution by the state assembly. This foundation of democracy was not always as well accepted as people believe.

Documenting the scene, the *Kline's Weekly Gazette* had harsh words for the protesters. Its report of January 2, 1788, was clearly biased: "Every lover of good order must lament the wound the dignity of this state has received in the burning in the public street…the effigy of the first magistrate of the Commonwealth."

The newspaper suspected many in the mob to be former British redcoats or fairly recent immigrants who, until that day, were ignored by local residents. Debate over the Constitution would spark no fewer than five public demonstrations on the streets of Carlisle.

Local residents had reason to distrust the government. The powers-that-be had ignored Indian attacks that had turned the town into a frontier refugee camp during the first decade of its existence. The refusal to give Cumberland and other western counties equal representation to that of Philadelphia and the eastern counties fueled local support of the Revolution.

A petition had circulated in Carlisle calling for the unanimous adoption of the federal Constitution, but up to 170 local residents signed an Antifederalist petition in opposition to ratification until a Bill of Rights was included. Antifederalists believed in state sovereignty and feared that individuals might be deprived of rights and liberties under the federal Constitution.

Sixty-nine delegates attended the Pennsylvania Convention in December 1787. Nine spoke in favor of the Constitution, including James Wilson, a former Carlisle resident and signer of the Declaration of Independence. Robert Whitehall, a Cumberland County delegate, moved that the convention be adjourned until amendments could be drafted to the proposed Constitution. His motion lost forty-six to twenty-three. The same vote split ratified the document, setting in motion a storm of protest.

Federalists in Carlisle organized a rally to celebrate Pennsylvania's ratification. At 5:00 p.m. on December 26, the courthouse bell rang signaling federal supporters to assemble in the square. A cannon was hauled from Foster's Tavern on North Hanover Street to the crossroads, where material was collected for a bonfire to be lit at dusk.

Not to be outdone, the Antifederalists gathered in opposition, carrying sticks, staves and clubs. They harassed the Federalists with shouts and insults. The newspaper reported that Major James Armstrong Wilson, son of Thomas Wilson, was preparing to have the cannon loaded when the armed men ordered him to stop. They threatened to hurt anyone who tried to light the bonfire.

The major suggested that the men leave if they were unwilling to celebrate. At that point, more jeers and insults were hurled at Major Wilson, along with sticks and staves. The *Gazette* reported the major was struck on the breast. Angry, Wilson lunged forward and struck a man with the stick holding the match rope. Wilson was immediately jumped by six or seven men, who beat him to the ground. The newspaper speculated that they would have killed the major had it not been for a trusty old soldier who threw himself on Wilson and took the blows.

Caught unprepared, the Federalists were forced to retreat, clearing the way for the Antifederalists to spike the cannon, light the bonfire and throw the cannon and its carriage into the flames. They sent for an almanac containing the Constitution and cheered as it burned. The *Gazette* reported loud cheers damning the forty-six delegates who had voted for ratification and praising the virtuous twenty-three who had opposed it.

The next day at noon, the Federalists tried again to rally on the square. This time, they were armed with muskets and bayonets to repel any attacks. While the Antifederalists hovered in the distance, "Friends of Government," as they called themselves, lit a bonfire and read aloud a copy of the resolution passed by the assembly to ratify the Constitution. This was followed by cheers, along with musket and cannon fire.

After celebrating for two hours, the Federalists retired to a local tavern, where they ate supper and offered up toasts to James Wilson, the "patriotic" forty-six, the Constitution and its rapid ratification by all states. Meanwhile, the Antifederalists held their own rally, which included the burning of the effigies.

The demonstrations were a source of debate for months. Some declared the *Gazette* article untrue. Prominent local leader John Montgomery called the write-up "a wicked, devilish piece." In a letter dated January 9, 1788, he described the tension in town:

> *There is no hope of accommodating this unhappy affair...Our situation is exceedingly disagreeable. Neighbors rubbing against each other as they pass and not a word spoken. Great pains are taken to influence the minds of the country people and there is now a great majority of them opposed to the new Constitution.*

On January 23, the state supreme court issued warrants for twenty-one Antifederalists involved in the riot that injured Major Wilson. The court decided to release the men on parole, but seven men insisted on a trial and refused bail, preferring jail instead.

On Saturday, March 1, the courthouse bell rang again and continued to peal through the morning as companies of militia marched into Carlisle from all parts of Cumberland County. By 10:00 a.m., Antifederalists had taken over the courthouse, and hundreds of people had assembled downtown. A meeting was held between militia officers and residents representing the Federalist and Antifederalist camps. It was agreed that prosecutors should recommend that the attorney general not press charges against the rioters.

Instead of returning home, the militiamen marched to the county jail, freed the prisoners and escorted them in triumph to the courthouse, where their discharges were read aloud to the cheers of the masses. John Shippen was in no mood to celebrate. In a March 3 letter to his father, Colonel Joseph Shippen, he described the crowd as a dirty mob of ragamuffin blackguards numbering close to eight hundred. His words spoke disdain for the Antifederalist cause:

> *It was feared they would all remain at night in town to do mischief, but their leaving in the afternoon produced an agreeable disappointment. It may seem strange they should be permitted to do as they pleased, but for want of a sufficient number to repel them, the gentlemen of town, who are men of sense and forethought, men of true courage, thought it most proper to let them alone.*

Shippen went on to say that Federalists in Carlisle could have raised two to three hundred well-armed men in response to the Antifederalists but opted to avoid a civil war. In the end, the First Congress amended the Constitution to include the Bill of Rights.

"The Sword of Justice"

Washington and the Whiskey Rebellion

The first casualty of any war may be empathy. Fife Major Samuel Dewees had to harden his resolve on the boat across the Susquehanna River to Carlisle and beyond. "Our country called, and duty was clearly spread out before our eyes," he wrote later. "We had, therefore, to steel our hearts against the cries of mothers and children, and brace up against the weeping and wailing by playing and beating up merrily 'Charley Over The Water.'"

Earlier, his unit had paraded through the streets of Harrisburg. Now it was off to the west to put down a frontier rebellion barely eleven years after the country had won its independence. Days later, Dewees waited for his cue as President George Washington passed down the line in review of his troops standing at attention on High Street in Carlisle. Officers out front saluted the commander in chief by bringing the hilt of their swords up toward their faces before throwing the points down toward the ground.

As Washington advanced, different musicians played different tunes based more on what they knew than what was proper. "Some drummers no doubt knew what tune was a salute and could have played it, but their fifers could not play it," Dewees wrote later. "Some fifers knew how to play it, but their drummers could not beat it." But Dewees and his drummer struck up the old "British Grenadier's March," which was always played as a salute during the Revolutionary War.

"President Washington eyed us keenly as he was passing us, and continued to do so, even when he had passed to some distance from us," Dewees wrote. Later, his commanding officer confirmed what Washington had already suspected. Dewees and his drummer had once served in the Continental army. The president was impressed that they had remembered and played a rendition as well as any heard during the war.

Not long after, the army marched out of Carlisle, ending a hectic week for Washington. It was October 11, 1794. The Whiskey Rebellion was underway. When the army formed for departure, the column stretched from West Street east to Gallows Ground, where York and Trindle Roads now intersect.

War with Britain added to the hatred people had for taxes, and many in the Cumberland Valley were familiar with the abuses of tax laws in Scotland and Ireland. The trouble was that revenue from imports was not enough to pay off Revolutionary War debt, sustain the government and support an army against the Indians. Congress passed a law on March 3, 1791, levying a tax on distilled spirits, figuring it a commodity of least necessity.

The tax was violently opposed by many in western Pennsylvania because they thought it was oppressive and unequal. The Constitution required that all taxes be uniform throughout the country, but opposition leaders felt that the new tax bore heavily on the only region where spirits were extensively manufactured.

Frontier farmers often produced large amounts of excess wheat, corn and rye for which there was no market. Instead of letting it go to waste, they would distill the grain into alcohol to make it more profitable and easier to transport in bulk over the mountains. In many parts of the frontier, every fifth or sixth farmer operated a distillery.

It was thought at first that the tax would not be enforced and would be repealed. Those against the tax discouraged its collection by intimidating tax agents and destroying their property. Mass meetings were held. Liberty poles went up in public places. Armed resistance was organized.

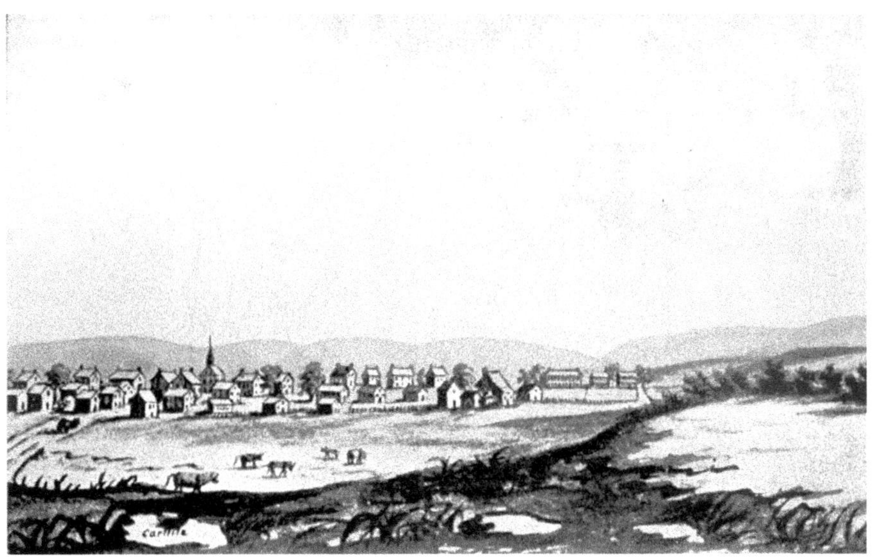

The earliest known sketch of Carlisle, drawn circa 1797. The steeple marks the first courthouse, and the old barracks are at right. *Courtesy of CCHS.*

Washington was angered by these attacks on a country he had fought so hard to create. He saw the insurgents as threats to domestic tranquility, general welfare and even posterity. On August 7, 1794, Washington issued a proclamation ordering the insurgents to disperse by September 1.

General William Irvine was sent west to negotiate terms with the settlers. On August 16, 1794, Irvine wrote that many in Cumberland County would take offense to his mission and use it against him, "but I make a rule of doing what I think is right and trust to events for consequences." The talks ultimately failed.

Prominent men in Carlisle were hopeful that a few court cases would show how unfair the law was and lead to it being changed or repealed. Reverends Charles Nisbet and Robert Davidson of the First Presbyterian Church urged local residents to express their views in a constitutional way while submitting to the authority of the law.

The people had other ideas. On September 8, 1794, protesters erected a liberty pole on the square with the words "Liberty and No Excise." The next morning, "friends of good government" took down the pole, but this only aggravated the situation.

"Runners were dispatched in every direction to inflame the minds of the country people and persuade them to assist in putting up a second pole,"

Conway Wing wrote in his history. Two days later, on September 11, 1794, two hundred armed men stormed into Carlisle and put up an even larger pole, this time reading "Liberty and Equality."

The mob reportedly roamed the streets for several days and nights, guarding the pole and keeping residents awake by shouting and firing guns at night. There were even cases in which the mob stopped local residents at the point of bayonet and demanded money to buy whiskey. Local farmers expressing outrage over the behavior were threatened with the destruction of property. Insurgents also threatened any militiamen who reported for duty.

One source reported that the wife of Colonel Ephraim Blaine, who was an invalid, had Blaine's sister ride into Carlisle each day to do housework and care for the family. The former commissary general of the Continental army was escorting his sister back home one night when they were attacked by Whiskey Rebels. The rebels pursued the siblings for two miles, firing several shots in their direction. None of the bullets hit target, and the pair escaped injury.

On September 25, 1794, Washington issued a proclamation ordering Pennsylvania, Virginia, New Jersey and Maryland to raise their militias and converge on Carlisle. Washington was to become the only standing president to personally lead soldiers into harm's way. Their target was four counties in western Pennsylvania where farmers were incited by men like lawyer and congressman William Findley.

Washington left Philadelphia for Carlisle on October 5, 1794. The next day, he forded the Susquehanna River and was met on the West Shore by the Philadelphia Light Horse. The cavalry unit then escorted the president west on what is now Route 11. In his journal, Washington called the land from Harrisburg to Carlisle "exceedingly fine, but not under such cultivation and improvement as one might have expected."

Two miles outside Carlisle, Washington was met by the governors of Pennsylvania and New Jersey. An officer from camp described how Washington, upon his arrival, pulled off his hat and bowed to the officers and men. The soldiers showed "the same affectionate regard that would have been to an honored parent."

Upon entering Carlisle, Washington passed in front of crowds gathered in the streets, silent in admiration for the president. The commander in chief then reviewed the ranks of artillery, cavalry and infantry troops gathered in front of their tents on the commons (public land outside the borough now occupied by Dickinson College and various neighborhoods).

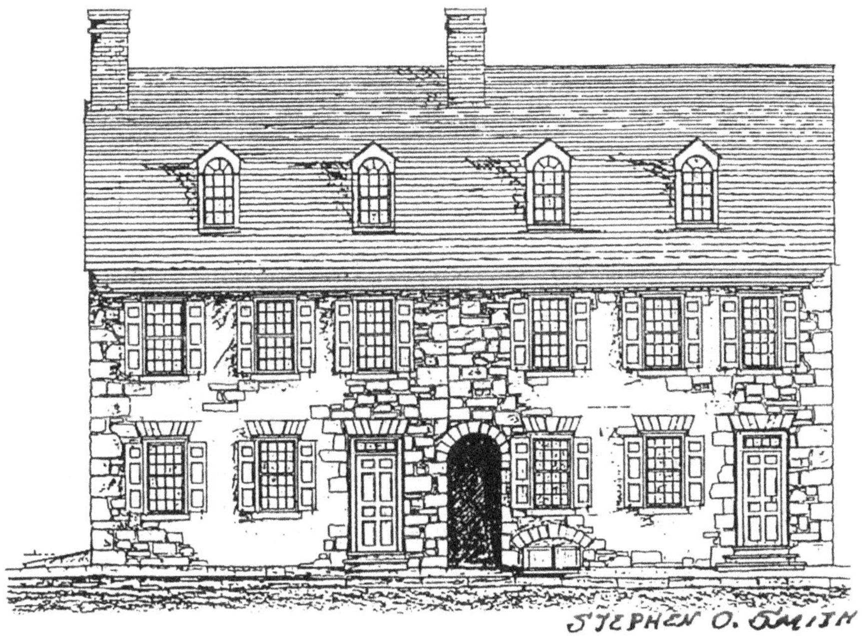

A sketch of the Blaine House by local architect Steve Smith. *Courtesy of CCHS.*

The next day, Washington heard Davidson preach a sermon at First Presbyterian Church. From October 6 to 12, the president was busy trying to organize and prepare the army. The president and his officers stayed at the Blaine house located at 1 and 5 South Hanover Street.

Between ten and fifteen thousand soldiers were in Carlisle. Local merchants welcomed them, figuring that they were good for the economy. When the soldiers had first arrived days before, the Whiskey Rebels drew away from Carlisle.

Large numbers of arms, ammunition and equipment were forwarded to Carlisle Barracks to be issued to soldiers as needed. Men from four states arrived on different schedules and in varying stages of readiness. They all had to be fed, equipped, marched to a unit and trained for the fight ahead.

As supply wagons rolled into town, Carlisle took on its familiar role as a military staging area. Officers were in town with their entourages of horses, wagons and trappings of station. This citizen army consisted of two distinct classes. Most officers came from the creditor aristocracy of seaboard cities and were eager for low-risk glory. The lower ranks were crowded with the poorest laborers and landless workers, recent immigrants and subsistence farmers. While officers had plenty to eat and drink and enjoyed warm beds in local taverns and homes, the rank and file soldiered on with poor rations and scarce blankets and tents.

Much time was spent dispatching search parties to find deserters. There were stories of drunken soldiers charging through fields of ripened crops, tearing down fences for firewood, slaughtering farm animals and sleeping where they fell. Two civilians were killed. A boy was shot by soldiers hunting suspects in the pole raising in Carlisle. A local drunk was stabbed by a bayonet during a tussle with soldiers he had mocked. The courts later found the deaths accidental and released the soldiers involved.

Washington pressed his officers to exercise better control over their men. Pennsylvania Governor Thomas Mifflin set a poor example by getting so drunk in Carlisle one night that he ordered the Philadelphia Light Horse to fire on all comers.

At one point, Findley came to Carlisle to meet with Washington and offer a message of conciliation. The president received Findley but sent him back west with the ultimatum that the army would march if the rebels did not disperse and pledge themselves to obey the law. Washington made sure that Findley saw the large army arrayed against the insurrection.

Before his departure, several prominent residents addressed Washington, expressing their appreciation for him and his legacy. While praising the "good and virtuous," they lambasted the "western insurgents" as "malevolent disturbers of the public peace." World history affords many instances where free governments have been destroyed by unprincipled men, their address read, "yet the present insurrection and opposition to government is exceeded by none, either for its causeless origin or for the extreme malignity and wickedness with which it has been executed."

The residents urged unity among all good men to restore order and punish those who have spurned "the most tender and humane affairs" for a resolution. The address went on to read: "The sword of justice in the hands of our beloved President can only be considered an object of terror by the wicked, and will be looked up to by the good and virtuous as their safeguard and protection."

Washington thanked them for their words, saying that he was pleased with their "enlightened and patriotic attachment…towards our happy Constitution."

"Let us hope the delusion cannot be lasting, that reason will speedily regain her empire," Washington said. "Let the wise and virtuous unite their efforts to reclaim the misguided."

Days were spent drilling the army. By October 10, 1794, Washington had deployed his covering force of light cavalry from New Jersey and Philadelphia to the west, followed the next day by his main body of troops. Upon approach of the army, rebel leaders sued for peace, and Governor Henry Lee of Virginia granted amnesty to all except the leaders who refused to take an oath of allegiance.

"The Work of an Incendiary"

The Courthouse Fire of 1845

There was a violent northwest wind on the morning that the Carlisle government was reduced to ash by a rapidly spreading fire that destroyed both the town hall and county courthouse. Only the heroic efforts of local residents, along with help from nearby Carlisle Barracks, prevented an even worse disaster.

Residents awoke to the cry of "Fire!" at about 1:00 a.m. on March 24, 1845. Flames were seen coming from the shed behind town hall, where three different volunteer fire companies kept their apparatus. The trouble was, the fire engines were tied so tightly together that it was impossible for firemen to pull equipment from storage to fight the fire. The *Carlisle Herald & Expositor* reported that the ground floor interior was entirely in flames. Crews managed to free one engine, but it was so damaged that it was declared unfit for use.

Eight-year-old John Hays was sleeping in a third-floor room of a nearby home when he was roused from bed by the commotion outside. He later wrote of that night in a letter to a friend dated 1914, when Hays was seventy-seven and president of the Frog Switch Manufacturing Co.

Hays said that when he opened his eyes, he saw his cousin hastily getting dressed. She advised him and his sister that the town hall was on fire. Being curious, the siblings went to a window facing the square. Hays recalled the scene:

> *The engine room doors on the ground floor were wide open and the room inside was ablaze. I could see the engines in it. A bucket line was completing its formation from the pump on the 1st* [Presbyterian] *church square.*

The *Carlisle Herald & Expositor* described the gravity of the situation:

> *The scene now presented an appalling prospect—with no fire apparatus, no means of arresting the mad career of the devouring element, the full destruction of the whole southeastern portion of the town seemed inevitable.*

From his vantage point, Hays saw Mr. Alexander come out of his home across the street and begin to take part in the bucket line on the square. Mrs. Alexander followed her husband out, brought him back to the house and then went up North Hanover Street to check on neighbors. By the time she returned, her husband was out again, but this time, when she took him back, she locked the door on him. Hays wrote how Mr. Alexander died four months later on July 30, but not from his prior illness or exposure on the night of the fire. Hays did not elaborate on the cause of death in his story about the overly protective wife.

As Hays continued to watch, flames went through the roof of town hall, and soon the county courthouse was also on fire. The buildings were only separated by a few feet. "Men on the roof succeeded in putting it out several times, but [the fire] grew too strong and too hot for them and they had to crawl back," Hays wrote. "We watched the fire spread out from the hip until the whole roof was on fire. Then the belfry burned and the bell went down."

Bystanders soon realized that there was no saving town hall or the courthouse, so they focused on saving nearby buildings on the southeast corner of the square. The *Carlisle Herald* reported that residents acted quickly to remove and secure records from various county offices as the courthouse burned. The documents were deposited in nearby homes to be collected later.

The *American Volunteer* had its newspaper office on the square behind the Old Market House, now the site of the modern courthouse. It reported how residents, using ladders to climb to roofs, carried buckets and laid down wet blankets to prevent sparks carried on the wind from touching off more fires. The bucket line of brave residents was assisted by the timely arrival of the fire engine from the artillery company at the barracks. By

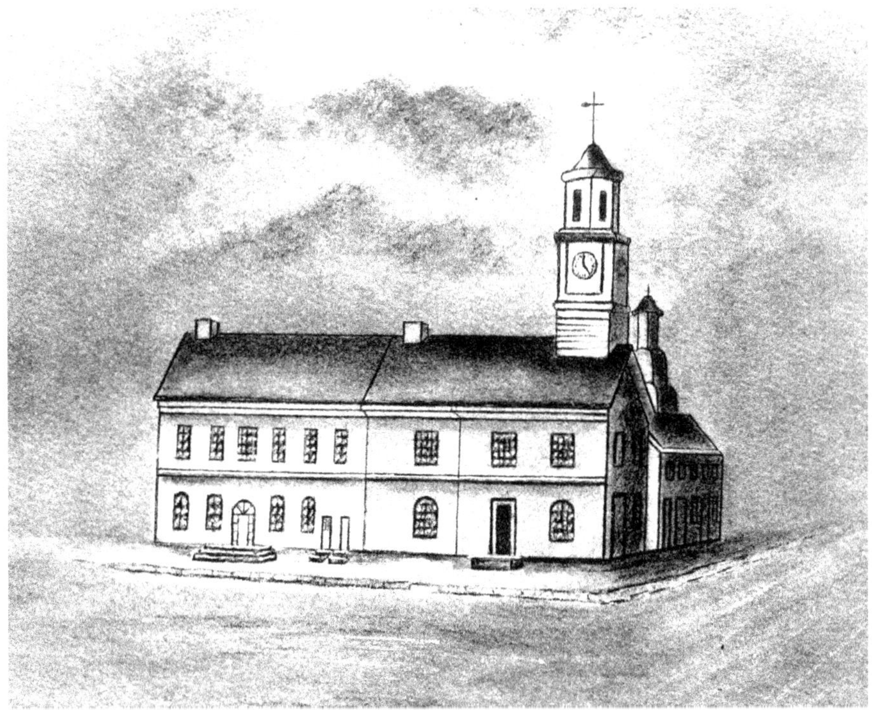

This sketch of the first courthouse and town hall shows how close the buildings were to each other. *Courtesy of CCHS.*

4:00 a.m., nothing remained of town hall or the courthouse but the clock bell and smoldering ruins, the *Volunteer* reported. Preliminary estimates put the loss at $35,000 to $40,000.

There was immediate speculation that the fire had been set by an arsonist due to the rapid spread of the flames and the fact that the fire engines were lashed tightly together. "[It] was thought to be the work of an incendiary," the *Carlisle Herald* reported. The *Volunteer* had some choice words for the villain: "We sincerely pray Heaven that the guilty wretch may yet be detected and brought to condign punishment." The Cumberland County commissioners offered a reward of $500 for information leading to the arrest of the arsonist, but nothing ever came of it.

Carlisle residents wasted no time. That evening, a town meeting was held to discuss how to rebuild the courthouse and accommodate public offices and records. Two committees were formed—one to lobby the state legislature for money to rebuild the courthouse and another to solicit donations to replace lost firefighting equipment.

Meanwhile, the county commissioners made arrangements with the local school district to hold courts in Education Hall in Church Alley just west of the square. One month later, the commissioners awarded a $40,000 contract to Wilt and Bryan of Harrisburg to construct a new building on the southwest corner of the square. That structure still stands and is known by locals as the Old Courthouse.

In the interim, important records were housed on Beetem's Row on South West Street between Pomfret Street and Chapel Alley. It was there that the county relocated many of its important offices. Fearful that documents might be scattered about town, the commissioners asked citizens to hand over the paperwork to the proper authorities.

A borough proposal in May to form a night watch was dismissed by the *Volunteer* as a ploy by Whig councilmen to squander some $600 to $800 a year on political supporters.

"My Presence...Was Purely Accidental"

The McClintock Slave Riot of 1847

It was hardly a ringing endorsement from his fellow Carlisle residents. When the Dickinson College professor entered the courtroom, whites in the audience muttered or shouted, "There goes McClintock...The damned abolitionist...Three groans for McClintock!"

Only minutes before, Reverend John McClintock was taking his daily walk to the post office at about 5:00 p.m. when postmaster George Sanderson told him of the habeas corpus hearing for fugitive slaves. The professor went over to the Old Courthouse to investigate, entering the second-floor courtroom just as Judge Samuel Hepburn ordered the release of three slaves held by the county sheriff into the custody of their owners.

As McClintock entered the courtroom, he met an Episcopal minister who expressed doubt that testimony offered at the hearing proved that the woman and child involved were slaves. What's more, state lawmakers had recently enacted a law banning any county court official from having any part in

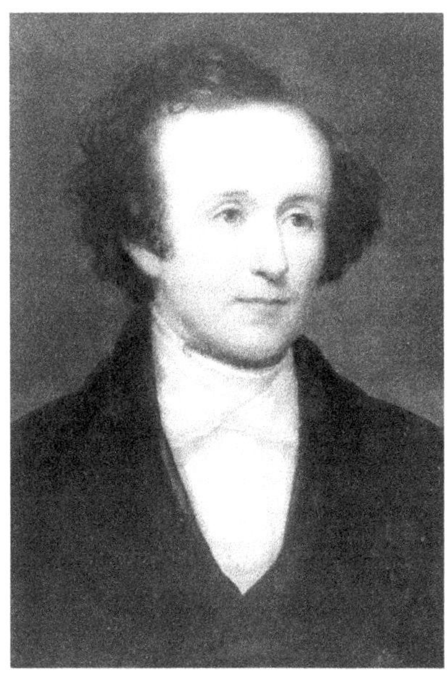

A portrait of John McClintock by James Barton Longacre, circa 1850. *Courtesy of CCHS.*

the recovery of fugitive slaves. The new law imposed a stiff fine on violators and put jurisdiction of fugitive slave cases exclusively on the federal government.

This rendered any proceeding held in Cumberland County court illegal. McClintock was the only person in court aware of the new law and the only person with access to a certified copy. So McClintock offered to retrieve his copy for the judge. It was June 3, 1847, and the professor was about to be mired in legal problems of his own.

In many ways, Carlisle of the mid-nineteenth century had more southern leanings than northern. Trade routes through the county went south and southwest. Southerners, particularly from Baltimore, spent summers at nearby resorts. Half of the Dickinson College student body was from the South, as were many of the officers stationed at Carlisle Barracks.

McClintock, meanwhile, had a reputation for being an outspoken critic of slavery. He saw its abolition as coming through religious reform in the attitudes toward it. "The church can do only one thing in regard to so heinous a crime as slavery, namely to bear her testimony against it, and use all her influence for its extirpation [destruction]," he once wrote.

Months prior to the hearing, the *Christian Advocate* published articles that McClintock wrote detailing how slavery had no basis in Scripture and was incompatible with Christianity. He wrote with such passion and force that he upset some readers to the point where the publication stopped running his articles.

History describes McClintock as possessing a quick intelligence, handsome features and a tendency to use sweeping gestures when making speeches. An ardent Whig, he had a lifelong interest in politics and an intense drive for work. His stance against slavery found little support in Carlisle. In his writings, McClintock made his position clear in relation to the criminal charges later pressed against him following a riot just outside the Old Courthouse:

> *The thrust of the case was my human and Christian sympathies were openly exhibited on the side of the poor blacks and this gave moral offence to the slave holders. The sentiment of the aristocracy of the town...is all pro-slavery...they are hand in glove with the lowest rabble.*

The confrontation began when two Hagerstown slave owners—James Kennedy and his brother-in-law, Howard Hollingsworth—came north to Carlisle to retrieve three fugitive slaves. It was alleged that Lloyd Brown and his ten-year-old daughter, Ann, belonged to Howard's father, Colonel Jacob Hollingsworth. Kennedy, meanwhile, wanted to claim a slave named Hester, who had married a Carlisle man. All three runaways were captured near Shippensburg before being transported to the county seat. At about noon on June 3, local Whig attorney Samuel Adair prepared a writ of habeas corpus for the release of the three fugitives held in county jail by the sheriff. The hearing was set for 4:00 p.m.

The *Herald* reported that testimony was offered identifying the slaves as the property of Hollingsworth and Kennedy. The newspaper explained that when attorneys asked the court to release the slaves, the judge granted the exceptions but discharged the slaves into the custody of the slave owners.

Sometime after 5:00 p.m., McClintock entered the courtroom, conferred with attorneys for the fugitives and advised the court on the new state law. The professor then left to get his certified copy.

During the hearing, Hollingsworth and Kennedy were put under arrest on a warrant accusing them of forcibly entering the house where the slaves had been found. As the two men left to give bail, they asked the county sheriff and his assistant to take charge of the fugitives. Incensed by this action, several local blacks in the audience rushed the prisoners' box to try to rescue Hester. The assistant sheriff drew his pistol and threatened to shoot anyone who attempted a rescue. Fearing a riot, the judge cleared the courtroom, forcing the crowd, except for the slaves and their captors, downstairs and outside.

As he left the courthouse, McClintock saw a white man raise a stick over the head of a black man, saying, "You ought to have your skull broke." The black man insisted that he had done nothing wrong. In his writings, the professor reported that he intervened, telling the black man, "If anyone strikes you apply to me, and I will see that justice is done to you."

Upon his return, McClintock stood on the front porch of the Old Courthouse talking with several young attorneys. A carriage had been pulled up against the building sidewalk. A short time later, the slave owners

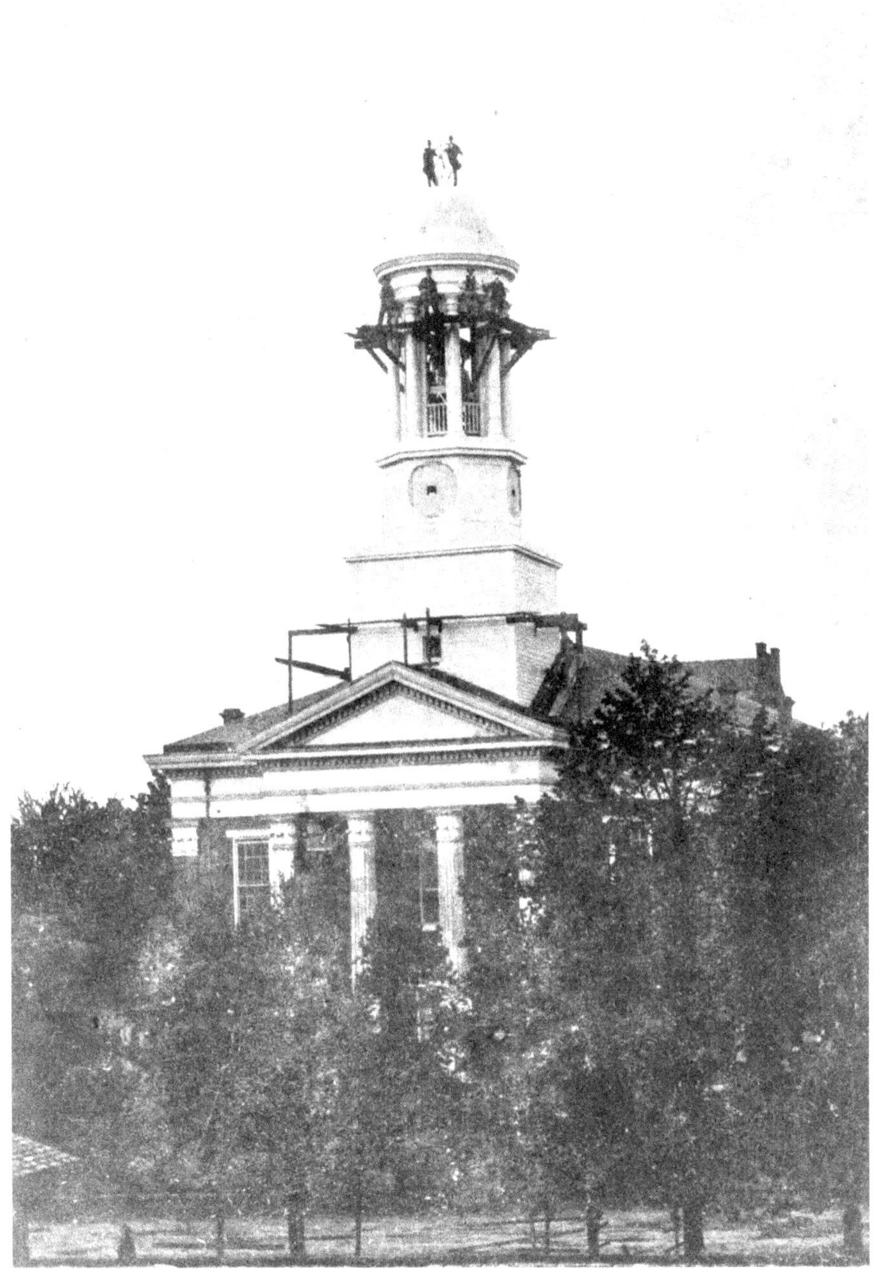

This photograph of the old county courthouse was taken circa 1865, when the top of the lantern was being repaired. *Courtesy of CCHS.*

and their slaves walked out of the courthouse heading for the carriage. The *Carlisle Herald* described what happened next:

> *Before the slaves got into the vehicle, a general rush was made on the slave owners and constables. A frightful melee ensued in the street...for some minutes, paving stones were hurled in showers and clubs and canes used with terrible energy.*

Free blacks made a rush for the woman and child. The crowd managed to carry them both away across to the other side of South Hanover Street. Kennedy pursued the crowd as it dashed down Liberty Avenue adjacent to what was then the site of the Carlisle Market House, now the modern courthouse.

Sources vary on what happened next. The *Carlisle Herald* reported that Kennedy was "felled to earth under a succession of blows from stones and clubs which completely disabled him." Another source reported that Kennedy had tripped on some boards lying on the sidewalk and was struck repeatedly by blacks as they rushed past him.

Wounded, Kennedy was carried back to his hotel. His injuries were severe—a badly bruised left arm, right hip and abdomen; a knee cap torn from its ligaments; and a bleeding wound on the back of his head. It was thought that Kennedy would recover, but he died suddenly about three weeks later, about June 25. Nothing appeared to connect his death directly to the injuries received in the riot.

The *Herald* reported that a boy named Black was hit in the head by a stone but soon recovered. His injuries were not as bad as people had originally thought. As word spread of the riot and injuries to Kennedy, many blamed McClintock for instigating the violence, claiming that he had cheered the blacks on and assured them that he would accept any consequences.

Soon a target of community anger, McClintock was arrested on charges of simple riot, assault and breach of the peace. The authorities also arrested thirty-four Carlisle-area blacks suspected of participating in the riot. That evening, the professor wrote a letter to his brother-in-law in which he described another instance where had he intervened on behalf of a black person:

> *An old negro woman called to me to save her from jail, as she had done nothing but to try to keep her old man from getting into the riot. I told the officer that if he carried her off illegally I should see her righted...All that*

I did was to try to do my duty to the laws of the land. But the slave catchers have spread abroad the report that I incited the riot. They will find that the saddle is on the wrong horse...Luckily, so far as I can learn, there is no man of the slightest character who can or will venture to swear against me, while there are scores who will testify on my side, that I did nothing to incite the riot.

A week later, on June 10, McClintock wrote to his father, trying to reassure his family of his innocence: "It is only another instance of the persecuting spirit of slavery and its abettors that this base attempt to injure me should thus foully be carried on...My presence at the courthouse was purely accidental."

Indeed, McClintock had friends among the townspeople, college faculty and student body, numbering just under two hundred in the 1840s. Almost one hundred students, most from the South, met on the chapel steps to adopt resolutions of confidence in McClintock. The college president paid the $300 in bail. But the college also engaged in damage control by sending letters to Dickinson supporters in the South to assure them that the professor was not an abolitionist and that his role in the riot was purely accidental.

The trial began on August 25, 1847, with McClintock as the chief defendant. From the start, the prosecution focused on convincing the jury to convict McClintock. Far less attention was paid to the other defendants, who occupied one side of the courtroom and were under the constant guard of court officers. Renowned abolitionist Thaddeus Stevens offered to take part in McClintock's defense.

Prosecution witnesses testified that the professor had incited the blacks to riot with such statements as "Go ahead boys, stand your ground" and "Now is your time. I'll see you through." One witness even described the professor as standing over the injured Kennedy and declaring that it served him right.

In a statement to the jury, prosecutors demanded a guilty verdict to appease the South and to make slave property secure. The fear was that once slaves believed they could get protection and aid from whites, their conduct would be marked by insubordination and violence:

If you decide these outrages can be committed with impunity, the foundation of the government would be broken, this union of states will be rent in twain...and the flare of a civil and, perhaps, of a servile war will light up the land. Your Southern brethren look to you, gentlemen of the jury, for

> *protection, and that by your verdict you will stay the lawlessness which threatens to overwhelm them.*

Public sentiment favored the prosecution at first, but sources report that the integrity, humanity and courage of John McClintock eventually won him acquittal. Judge Hepburn protested the verdict, reminding jurors when he cleared the courtroom that the line was drawn between what was peaceful and what was disorderly.

The judge said that when McClintock told the blacks to stand their ground, he became at that instant a rioter as guilty as those who committed the actual violence. But the truth was, court officers had provoked the riot by agreeing to keep the runaway slaves in custody even after they were remitted to the slave owners.

THE GRAY STORM TIDE

Without a doubt, Gettysburg was among the most decisive battles of the American Civil War. The sheer scope of this epic battle tends to overshadow the events leading up to it, along with the real objective of the Rebel invasion of 1863. Yet Carlisle and the whole Cumberland Valley found itself in the direct path of the Army of Northern Virginia, which had set its sights on the capture of Harrisburg. The following sections tell the story of Carlisle residents who were caught up in the gears of two war machines, along with a postwar story of healing old wounds.

"A Resigned Courage"

Rebel Occupation of Carlisle

There was a scene of perfect peace on East Street in Carlisle—a special moment when North and South were united as one by the futility of war and its many unanswered questions.

James Sullivan, a boy of fifteen, was a witness as neighbors gathered around Rebel soldiers camped out on their block for the evening meal. To make fires for supper, the enemy used telegraph poles that they had cut down earlier in the day to disrupt Union communications. A street pump supplied water for cooking.

The first wave of civilians were curious boys who surrounded the Rebels and fired off questions. Confederate soldiers answered in a civil, almost gentle way and within thirty minutes befriended the youths. Next came mothers, who only hours before had been terrified of the invaders. These women only wished to express their hope for a swift end to the war. Such was the peaceful scene when the cute girls arrived to stand by as their mothers listened to what the enemy soldiers had to say.

A pacifist Rebel asked the most basic questions—"How did this war get started, anyway? What was it all about?" Sullivan reported that no one had an answer, but everyone agreed not to repeat the "political claptrap" of either side at this peaceful gathering. Instead, East Street residents mourned their dead as the Rebels spoke of their own dreadful losses. "The heart of everyone in our little circle about the camp fire was melted," Sullivan later wrote. "Women silently wept."

It had been quite a different scene weeks before the Rebel occupation, when farmers throughout the Cumberland Valley fled through town in the wake of the 1863 invasion. Refugee families came and went, grimly riding this tide of war, heading east for safety beyond the Susquehanna River. Sullivan wrote:

> *The men and boys pegged along like tramps. The women and children, peering from their poor vehicles, seemed frightened dumb. They rarely took up talk with the townspeople, who gazed at them. I remember them as never singing, or calling, cheerily or otherwise, to one another, or shouting at the animals. The small children neither laughed nor cried.*

Two New York regiments had arrived in Carlisle on June 23 after retreating from Chambersburg and Shippensburg. Union soldiers prepared defenses west of town on Walnut Bottom Road and what is now the Ritner Highway. Carlisle formed its militia companies, and pickets were sent out in anticipation of battle. At about 1:00 a.m. June 24, Union general Joseph Knipe learned that Rebel forces were only two miles outside of town. He concluded that the enemy was too strong for the defenses, so he issued an order directing his troops to retreat to Harrisburg .

Word of the Rebel advance rattled prominent Carlisle citizens, prompting them to leave the town on foot or by whatever means they could find. They were joined on the crowded roads by farmers from the upper end of the county who had sought refuge for their livestock in and around Carlisle. Deputy Sheriff Simpson K. Donavin wrote that this only added to the alarm and confusion.

Carlisle residents went to bed on June 25 convinced that the Rebels would be in town by morning. "But the day dawned and the old town was more than usually quiet," Donavin wrote. "Citizens met each other with a smile and talked about the 'big scare.'"

Friday, June 26, passed without incident, as people relaxed upon hearing reports that the Rebels were still miles outside of Carlisle. By Saturday morning, June 27, it was difficult to find anyone willing to believe the rumors, but later that day, Union cavalry pickets had confirmed that they were true. The enemy was on the way. Donavin later wrote about the mood of the people:

> *There was calmness amounting almost to indifference, and a resigned courage that was more than virtue prevailing everywhere…If it was essential that this beautiful valley should be offered up to destruction, so as to save the Army of the Potomac, or give its commander time to mass his forces, it would have been offered.*

As the Rebels closed in, Colonel William Penrose and local officials rode out to meet with Confederate general Albert Jenkins. Penrose assured Jenkins that there were no Union forces in town and no resistance would be made. To spare panic among women and children, it was decided that the Rebel troops would march rather than charge into Carlisle. With so many false alarms, shouts of "the Rebels are coming" became like the old fable of the boy who cried wolf. So when the enemy actually marched into town, many had to see for themselves the Rebel army.

Sullivan recalled how his mother, peeping out the window, acted on impulse and went outside to satisfy her curiosity. He told her not to go, as did neighbors, who called out to her from behind window curtains, urging her to quickly return to safety. Sullivan went out and stood by his mother as they looked west up what is now High Street and saw a cavalry troop in close formation move toward them. The silhouette of the front rank of soldiers was outlined against the sky. The only sound was the clatter of hooves.

Fearful, his mother shrieked and ran back home, locking the front door and bolting the shutters. She feared for her daughter, whom she hid away. Sullivan stood his ground and watched the Rebels approach. He described them in his journal of war memories: "Big men, wearing broad brim hats,

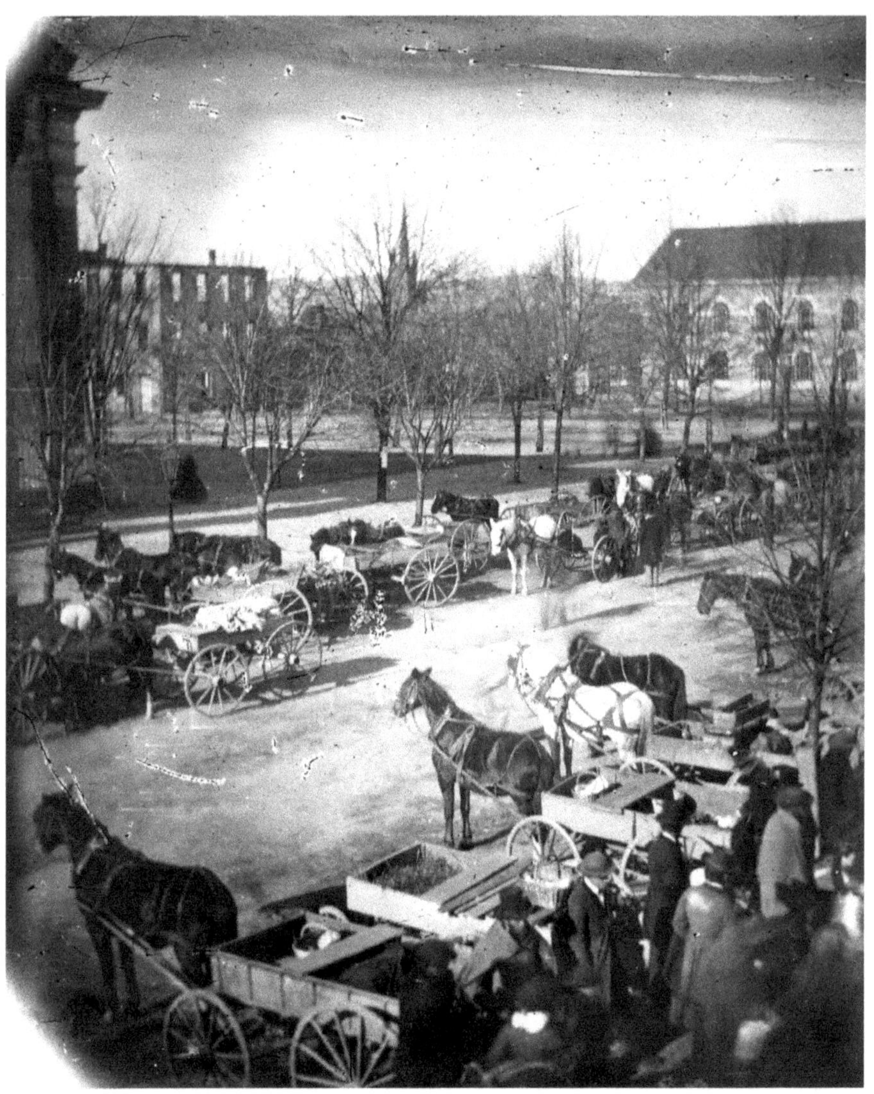

This page and opposite: These views of the square in Carlisle were taken on a market day, circa 1865. The market house is on the right. *Courtesy of CCHS.*

and mounted on good horses, they had a picturesque air of confidence and readiness for action." Later, on that first day of occupation, a company of infantry marched into the block and camped in the street hours before that night's peaceful scene.

Confederate cavalry had entered Carlisle from the west end of High Street at about 11:00 a.m. on Saturday. They advanced east to what are

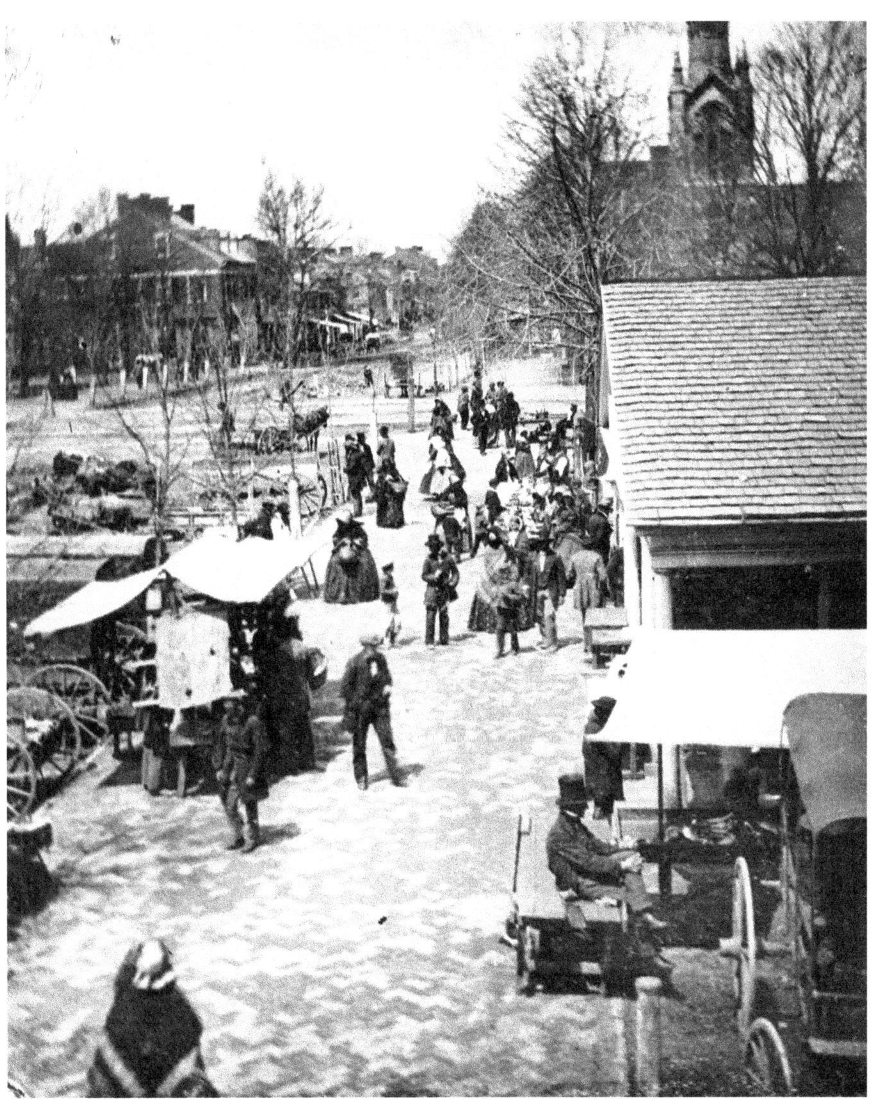

now Trindle and York Roads. One column split off to head for Carlisle Barracks before the main force returned to the square. There, Jenkins met with town officials and demanded that fifteen hundred rations be deposited within an hour at the Market House, where the modern county courthouse now stands. Otherwise, his men would help themselves to whatever food they could find.

Chief Burgess Andrew Ziegler, along with other citizens, went through town informing residents of the demand and requesting that each family furnish a share. Less than an hour later, the market house stalls were piled with food, and Rebel soldiers were lining up for grub. At 5:00 p.m. on Saturday, June 27, a band playing "Dixie" heralded the arrival of General Richard Ewell's corps by way of the Walnut Bottom Road, down South Pitt Street to High Street and then on to Carlisle Barracks by way of Bedford Street. Donavin described the Rebel soldiers:

> *The men of the command presented a sorry appearance. Many were barefooted, others hatless, numbers of them ragged, and all dirty. But they exhibited a cheerfulness which was indicative of great spirit and endurance.*

Within an hour, Confederate officers filled downtown streets and hotels or rode quietly through Carlisle. Some paid their respects at the homes of Carlisle residents they had met while stationed at the barracks. Donavin reported how most acted like gentlemen and were careful to restrain any bitterness they had toward the North, its people and their customs. He wrote:

> *It was only necessary to use the slightest insinuation that they were intruders to elicit a glowing, in some instances eloquent description of the desolation which had swept over parts of the South, and the suffering which their people had undergone.*

In hearing them talk, Donavin learned that they were tired of war and only continued fighting to be "left alone" by the North. Many were confident that their forces would capture the Army of the Potomac and, in turn, could seize both Baltimore and Washington, D.C. Meanwhile, Ewell set up his headquarters at Carlisle Barracks and dispatched an aide to Carlisle with a demand for more supplies, medicine and amputating tools.

Donavin reported that Carlisle residents thought the requisition was ridiculous and far beyond what they could supply. The Rebels, for example, wanted fifteen hundred barrels of flour from a town where there were barely two hundred barrels in stock. Other supplies requested by Ewell included twenty-five thousand pounds of bacon, five thousand pounds of coffee, three thousand pounds of sugar and one hundred sacks of salt.

Surgeons in town were required to bring their instruments to the Rebels. Local physician David N. Mahon came to the square with a handful

Hd. Qrs. 2d Corps
June 27th 1863

To the Authorities of Carlisle Pa
By direction of Lt. Genl
Ewell Comdg. You are requested
to furnish the following
subsistence for this Army

25000 lbs Bacon
100 Sacks Salt
1500 Bls. Flour
25 Bls. Potatoes
25 Bls. Molasses
3000 lbs. Coffee
3000 lbs. Sugar
25 Bls. Dried Fruit

The above supplies will be
ready at 6 O'clock, &
delivered at the front of the
Court House

W. J. Hawks, Maj &
C. S. 2d Corps

The original requisition
upon the Authorities of the
Borough of Carlisle. Pa, during
the confederate raid – June 27, 1863

The list of requisitioned supplies made by Confederate general Richard Ewell during the occupation of Carlisle on June 27, 1863. *Courtesy of CCHS.*

of antiques, which the Southern army doctor rejected after conducting an inspection. Shoes and cooking utensils were also requisitioned, along with such medical supplies as quinine and chloroform, which Carlisle could not provide.

The Rebels demanded that all of the items be placed in front of the Old Courthouse by 6:00 p.m. on Saturday. Borough officials were advised that failure to comply would mean homes and stores would be searched come Sunday morning until the supplies were found. Saturday night passed peacefully as enemy soldiers slept on the ground in and around Carlisle Barracks. Many lacked blankets and tents and were exposed to the elements.

Sunday morning, June 28, saw squads of soldiers appear on the streets to search homes, stores and warehouses for requisition items. The squads were preceded by prominent citizens calling upon homeowners not to show resistance if searched. Donavin suspected that the enemy had help from local residents who informed on their neighbors. He noted that often a Rebel squad went directly to a particular home to demand specific items. Donavin was convinced that this was only possible if the enemy had inside information. While he never mentioned names, he labeled the traitors "worse than the rebels" for their "villainous, dastardly work" and vowed that an outraged public would hold them accountable. Some supplies were from stores and warehouses, but none was from dwellings. Donavin said that the officers commanding the squads were polite and acted like gentlemen.

On Monday morning, June 29, Carlisle residents learned that the Rebel army had been ordered by high command to leave that afternoon. For two days, communications with Harrisburg had been cut off, leaving local residents unaware of events elsewhere in Pennsylvania. In his writings, Donavin described the mood among fellow citizens: "A painful anxiety was felt by all…There were a thousand rumors afloat. The very air was heavy with them, and the people with a patience that was a virtue, suffered and waited."

By 8:00 a.m. on Tuesday, June 30, most of the Rebel army had left Carlisle, bound eventually for the epic Battle of Gettysburg. About two hundred cavalry remained until Tuesday night on provost duty. Donavin reported that Ewell had intended to destroy the barracks but was talked out of it by local women who had been friends of his when he was stationed at Carlisle some years ago. After Ewell left, a crowd of "lewd and depraved men and women" plundered the barracks, destroying furniture and stealing any clothing and blankets they could find.

"The Rebels had not disturbed any of the records of the post, but the prostitutes and their friends did not consider anything sacred," Donavin wrote. "Blank leaves in the ledgers were torn out, and the paper generally scattered in any direction. The place was made thrice more desolate by this advent of thieves."

For much of Tuesday, Carlisle residents were upbeat. The enemy had left, and for a few hours there was relative calm, until about 2:00 p.m. when about four hundred Confederate cavalry entered the town from the direction of Dillsburg. Within half an hour, these men had procured alcohol and started to tear through the streets, cussing and yelling and "playing the demon."

Fed-up residents visited Colonel James Cochran and asked him to restrain his men. The commander assured them that his soldiers would behave under General Ewell's orders and not cause further trouble. Later that night, Jenkins returned to Carlisle after leading his men in the occupation of Mechanicsburg and probing Union defenses on the West Shore of the Susquehanna River. Carlisle residents welcomed Jenkins, who promptly dispatched squads to gather up the "drunken demons" commanded by Cochran.

"A Disagreeable Surprise"

The Shelling of Carlisle

At sunrise on Wednesday, July 1, cavalry under Captain William Boyd entered Carlisle amid the cheers of civilians anxious to hear news. He had none, except that his men were hungry, so local residents went into their homes and, within minutes, had food ready on the square to feed the soldiers. The troops rested briefly before setting out again in search of the enemy.

At 6:30 p.m., Union general William Smith entered Carlisle with three infantry regiments and about one hundred cavalry. Smith was greeted with joy, but he ignored the celebrations in favor of selecting the best artillery position to defend the town. Local boy James Sullivan was in the crowd watching the Union soldiers as they marched from Harrisburg Pike south

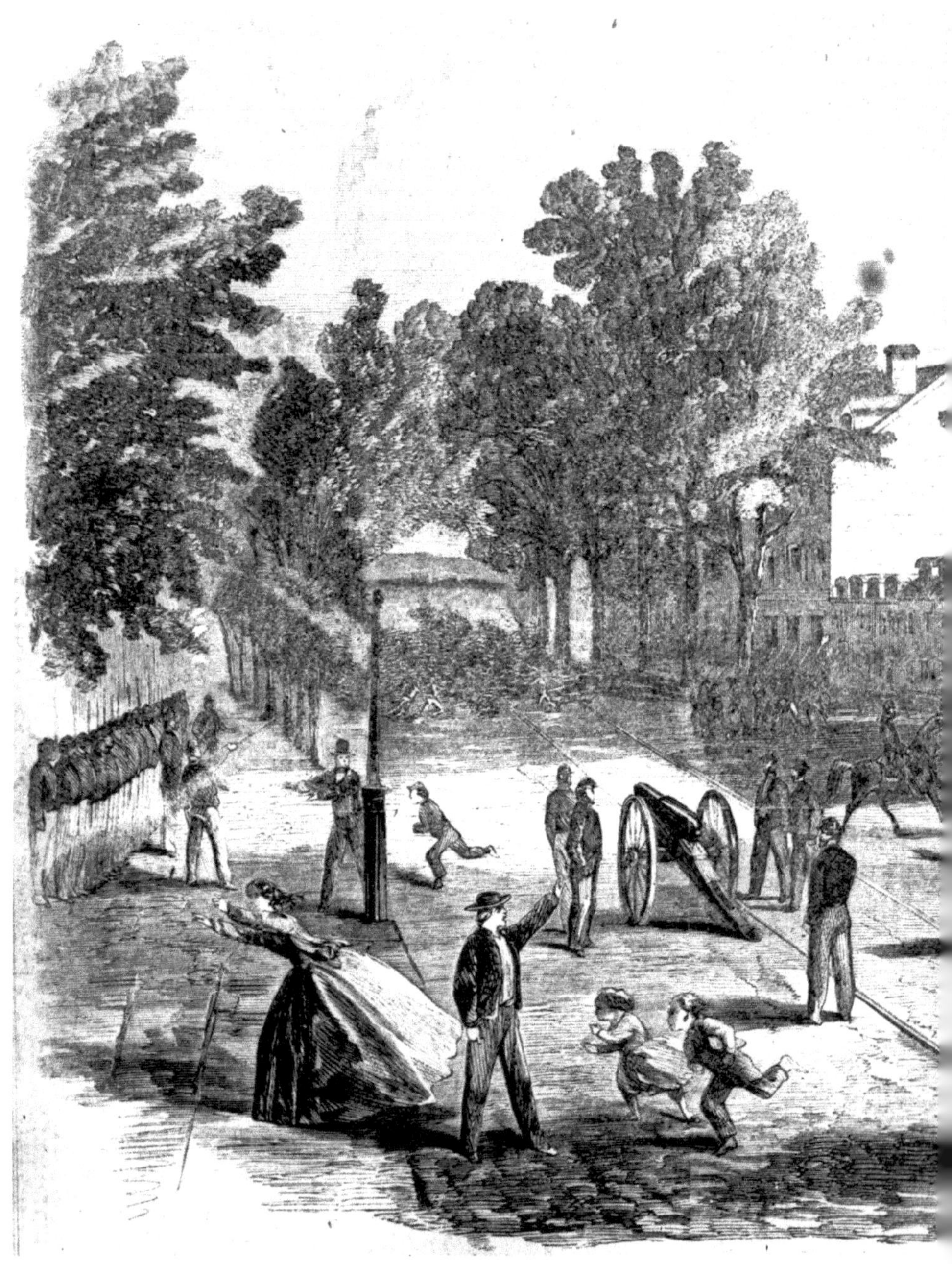

This scene of the first block of East High Street during the Confederate shelling was sketched by Thomas Nast. The market house is on the right. *Courtesy of CCHS.*

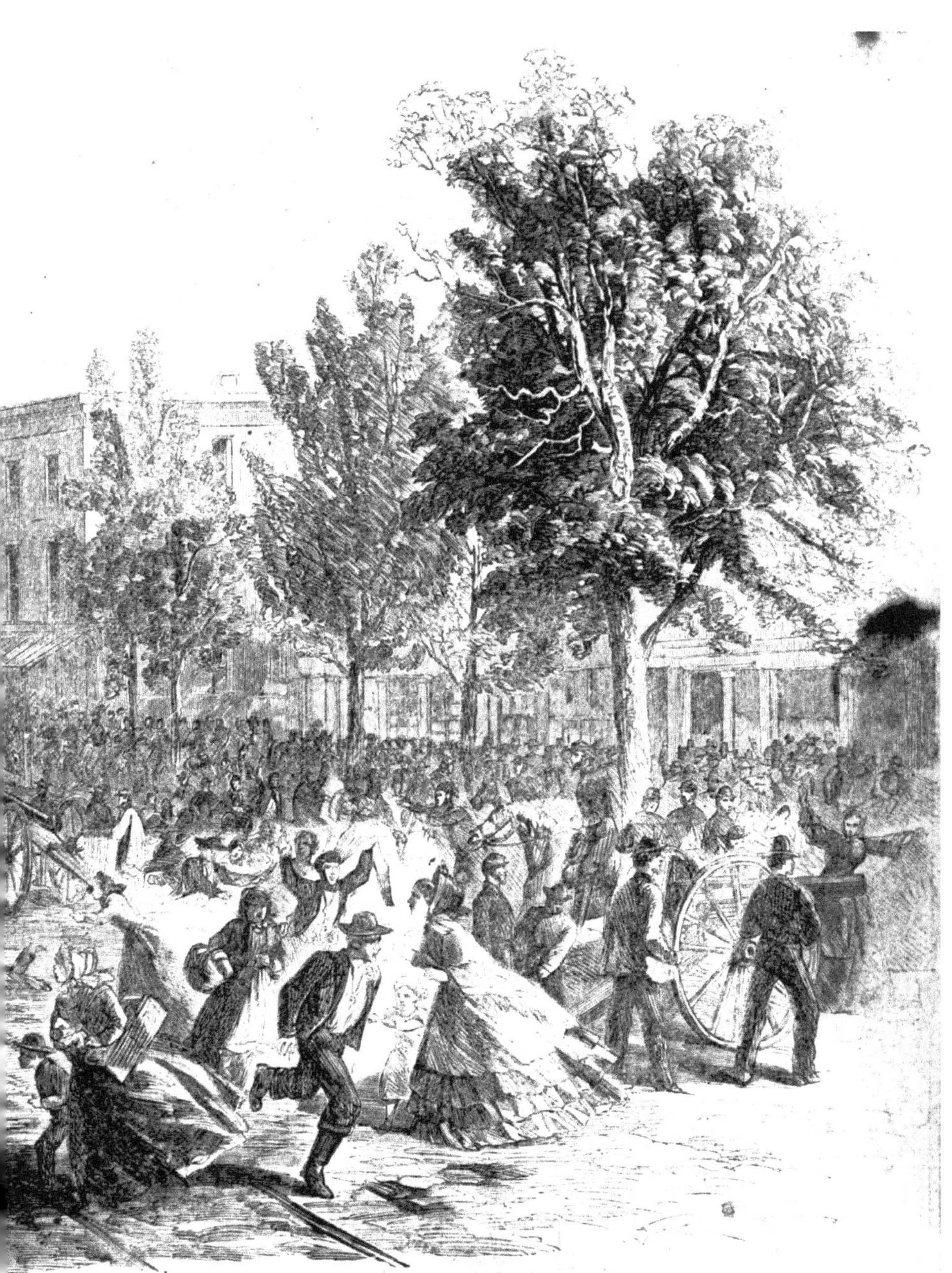

down Hanover Street to the square, where grateful civilians waited. He later wrote: "The women of Carlisle had brought out from their scantily stocked larders the essentials of a welcoming reception. Soon the scene was that of a merry picnic on a large scale."

Hungry from the long march, the soldiers stacked their arms on the town streets and sat on benches in front of the Market House enjoying the hospitality. Sullivan wrote how the celebration only lasted about half an hour before shouts of alarm were heard amid the laughter and busy talk. Donavin reported that at about 7:00 p.m., a body of cavalry was spotted at the junction of Trindle Spring and York Roads. He wrote that the formation came within two hundred yards of the town before it was identified as hostile:

> *They sat in their saddles, gazing up the street at the stacked arms of the infantry. I thought it was impossible that they could be rebels. The effrontery and boldness they exhibited was well calculated to create disbelief.*

Donavin was a believer within minutes. He blamed the sudden turn of events on lax precautions, saying that Union infantry had failed to throw out any pickets. The cavalry force under Boyd was operating behind the main body of the Rebels. Donavin described the ensuing firefight:

> *There was a call to arms…Companies of town militia, each man on his own account, hurried to the eastern section of the town, and selecting secure positions, opened a very telling fire on the force, which compelled them to fall back.*

The sudden appearance of enemy forces crashed the party downtown and created a panic among soldiers and civilians alike. Local girl Maggie Murray described the chaos in the square:

> *Such a stampede of women and children, you never saw in your life. You cannot imagine the confusion that ensued. It was a disagreeable surprise. Officers calling to their men, who were scattered in all directions, some eating, others worn out with their long march, fast asleep on the Square, and pavements.*

Sullivan described how Union soldiers scrambled to form up their units and retrieve weapons stacked just west of the Old Courthouse. In the confusion, the teenage boy did not know at first what was happening, so he ran beside a soldier and asked, "What's the matter?" The reply was: "The Rebels are right on us down by the railroad bridge coming into town."

If that was true, the enemy had already overrun the neighborhood where Sullivan lived. He last saw his mother and sister around the Market House on the southeast corner of the square, across the street from the Old Courthouse. The crowd had scattered within minutes of the first alarm, so there was no other sign of soldiers or civilians within the square. A cry had gone up for women and children to seek shelter in nearby cellars.

Maggie and her sister, Mary, ran up the alley beside First Presbyterian Church to a stable on Pitt Street about a block away. At one point, Maggie suggested that they head over to West High Street to see if the Rebels were in sight and if Union soldiers were drawn up in line of battle. Looking east down High Street, Maggie Murray saw a shell whizzing over her position. The sisters ran for home about two blocks away, chased by artillery fire. Maggie wrote later: "We never dreamed… the Rebel demons would attempt to shell the town…without giving the usual warning. The shot and shell was coming thick and fast. We all retreated to the cellar."

Meanwhile, Sullivan had seen an officer with the Seventy-first New York Regiment assemble his company between the Old Courthouse and High Street. The officer ordered his men to discard their packs on the sidewalk. Sullivan and two other boys were then asked by an officer to haul the packs over to a nearby building and toss the packs down the basement stairs. "The work proceeded rapidly," Sullivan wrote later. "All the packs of the regiment were coming to us it seemed. I handled so many. The last were heavy!"

That work done, Sullivan walked down an alley to Pitt Street and then on to West Street by way of Pomfret Street. By then, the shelling had stopped, and Sullivan decided it was time to head down an alley to his home on East Street. "Hardly any people were in the cross streets! I saw no soldiers; I imagine them disposed in defense as strategy dictated." At the southwest corner of East and High Streets, Sullivan came across two residents looking down the road. "There comes a flag of truce," one told him.

"A hundred yards down the street, slowly advancing toward us in the gathering darkness, were three horsemen," Sullivan wrote. "The officer bore on a staff held sidewise, horizontally, plainly visible to us, a white flag of quite a large size." When the enemy soldiers were between Spring and East Streets, two Union soldiers came out from behind a partly destroyed railroad pier and ordered them to halt. They were escorted past where Sullivan stood, moving west on High Street.

Donavin reported that the Rebel officer was taken to Smith's headquarters on Hanover Street. There, the enemy told the Union commander that Confederate brigadier general Fitzhugh Lee had a force of three thousand cavalry and demanded the unconditional surrender of Carlisle. Smith refused. When the Rebel officer told him that the shelling would proceed, Smith reportedly said, "Shell away."

No time was offered to evacuate women and children, and by then, word of the truce had circulated through town. A scene of confusion followed as civilians, weary of the shelling, decided to leave Carlisle.

"In a few minutes, the streets presented a sad and lamentable picture," Donavin wrote. He described a scene of mothers carrying their babies, while other children clung to them weeping and moaning. Meanwhile, the sick and those scarcely able to walk were carried by friends as old and young moved side by side, trudging toward the open country north of town. The Murray family was among those who evacuated town.

Upon reaching his home, Sullivan found his sister and mother, who had decided to evacuate her children, convinced that the Rebels would renew their bombardment. She collected some sleeping garments and rushed her children west on High Street. "It was not quiet; few persons were to be seen," Sullivan wrote later. "We moved slowly, at mother's pace. We had reached but a short distance west of the Square when a lively firing…began again. No truce had been agreed upon."

Shelling commenced a short time after the Rebel officer returned to the lines. Donavin described how this volley was "fiercer, heavier and more devilish" than the first. The streets, by this time, were crowded with people. "Shells flew thicker and grape and canister [shot] raked the streets incessantly," Donavin wrote. "Women and children ran into the dwellings and secreted themselves in the cellars, where they in terror listened to the hellish carnival."

Sullivan noticed that, within thirty seconds, local residents had cleared the streets again, except for his family. His mother was determined to reach a friend's house farther uptown. "A shell exploded with deafening force back by the First Presbyterian Church; another across the street from us; several near, both to the east and west."

A man, watching the family from the shelter of an alley, yelled at them to take cover. "For God's sake, woman, take the children off the street. Do you want all to be killed?" Mother Sullivan heeded the advice, and the family took cover in the basement of a home on Pitt Street next to

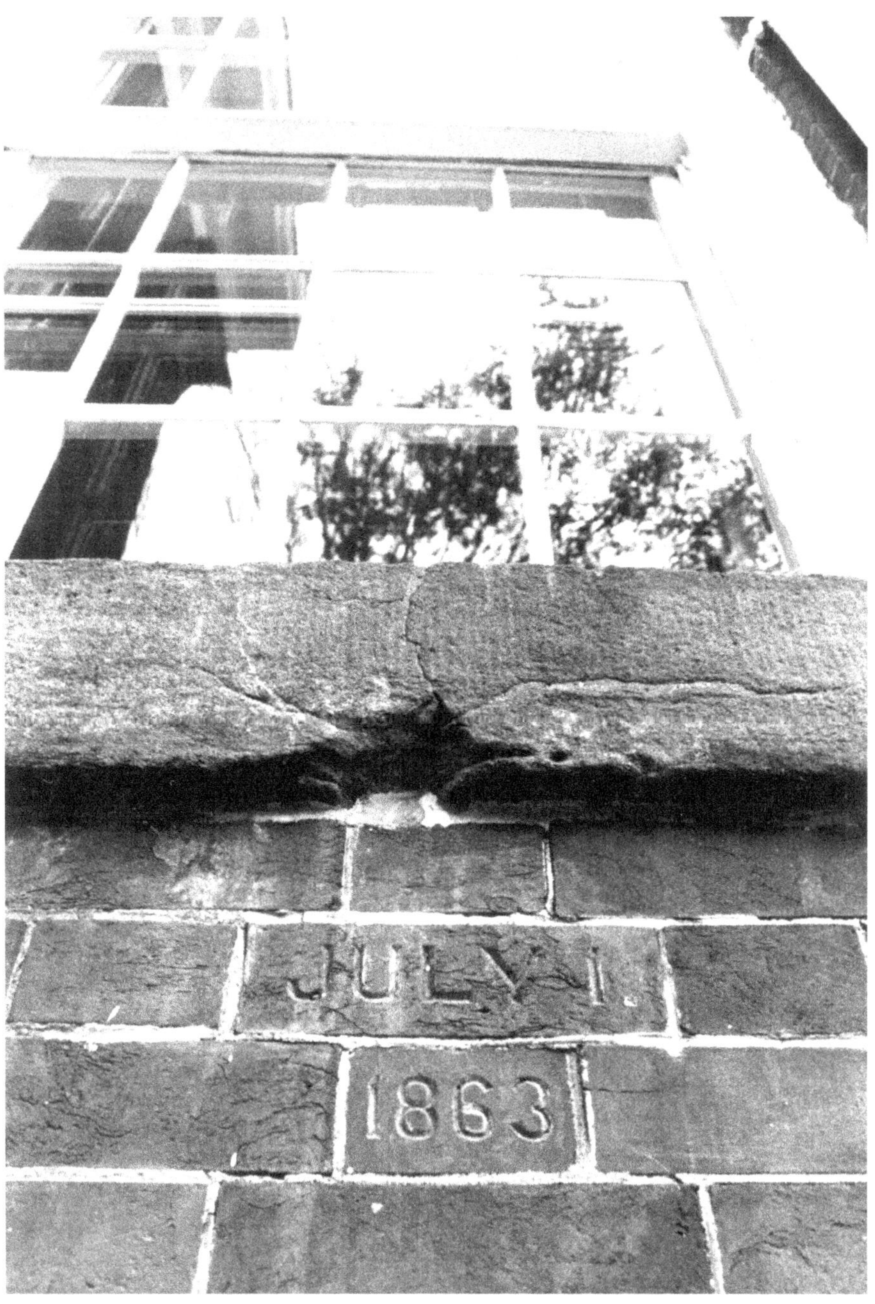

This 1997 photo by Jim Bradley depicts a scar from the Confederate shelling under one window of the Old Courthouse. *Courtesy of CCHS.*

the Methodist Church. There, they weathered the storm with the home's occupants and several other refugees until the firing stopped.

Mother Sullivan then decided to lead her family back home. They arrived after 10:00 p.m. to find debris in and around the parlor chimney and a coating of mortar dust all over the room. An enemy shell had hit the chimney in the attic, causing brick and stone to fall down the flue. Two other shells had passed through the home without exploding. "Mother's screams betrayed her fears that the house—her home for fifty years—was about to fall. Her trials during that day of feverish excitement had been too much for her. She wept and wailed."

Men from the neighborhood inspected the Sullivan home and found no evidence of immediate danger. The home served as a shelter the rest of the night for the Sullivan family and others living in that part of town. The scene was only made more terrifying when the Rebels set fire to Carlisle Barracks and a lumberyard on the east side of town. Residents there feared the worst, but no homes were put to the torch.

"Hungry Flames, Dead Silence"

The Burning of Carlisle Barracks

The Rebels put Carlisle Barracks to the torch at about 10:00 p.m. Within an hour, a great sheet of flame could be seen spreading over the sky in the northeast. Deputy Sheriff Simpson K. Donavin witnessed the burning and fumed over the monster he called Fitzhugh Lee. It was not enough that the Confederate brigadier general had shelled Carlisle.

"The hungry flames shot their red tongues high into the Heavens," Donavin wrote later.

> *Their mad fury could be heard amidst the roar of the artillery. Just when this scene of fire was grandest, the artillery ceased and a flag of truce bearer*

> *entered the town, and proceeded to Gen.* [William] *Smith's headquarters, where he renewed the demand for surrender.*

Donavin reported that Smith's response was more decided than courteous. Smith told the bearer to inform Fitzhugh Lee that he would sooner see him in a hotter climate first. It was during this lull that James Sullivan must have looked out the rear second-story window of his home on East Street.

"I looked northeast and east over open plots and fields," Sullivan recalled. He could see the flames from Carlisle Barracks half a mile away. Much closer was the fire at a lumberyard. "This spectacular destructiveness was going on without the slightest noise, not a shot was to be heard. The dead silence enhanced the impressiveness of the scene."

Donavin reported that the shelling commenced a third time once the truce bearer returned to the Confederate lines. This time, it didn't last as long. About 3:00 a.m., the Rebels fired three parting shots and "the fiend and his command" left by way of the Boiling Springs Road, Donavin wrote. Recalling events later, the deputy sheriff had only venom for the Confederate brigadier general who would return to Carlisle decades later:

> *It is supposed that from a want of ammunition and not of desire, this monster Lee ceased the bombardment…If he should ever fall into the hands of Union soldiers, as we most devoutly hope he may, let mercy such as he showed be meted out to him.*

In an after-action report, General J.E.B. Stuart described how he had received orders to move his cavalry command toward the Susquehanna River via Carlisle and Gettysburg. Pushing north, on the morning of July 1 Stuart reached Dover, York County, where he had hoped to meet up with General Jubal Early's division of Ewell's corps, but he learned that that division had moved on to Shippensburg. After some rest, Stuart pushed on to Carlisle by way of Dillsburg, hoping to link up with the Confederate army there.

"Our rations were entirely out," Stuart wrote.

> *I desired to levy a contribution on the inhabitants* [of Carlisle] *for rations, but was informed before reaching it that it was held by a considerable force of militia who were concealed in the buildings, with the view to entrap me upon my entrance into town.*

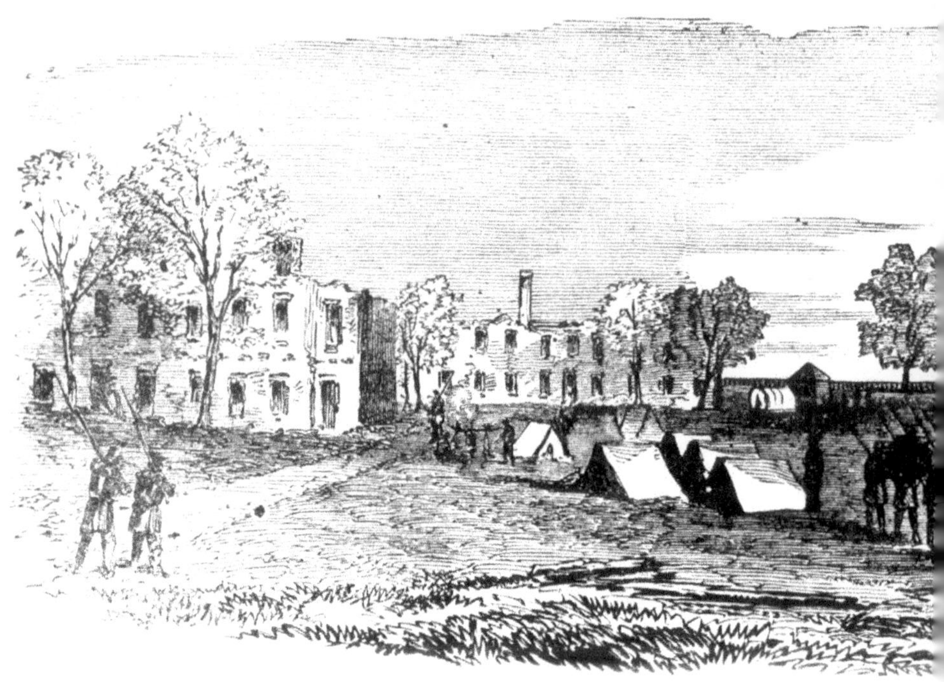

This sketch by George Law depicts General Smith's headquarters (right) and the ruins of Carlisle Barracks. *Courtesy of CCHS.*

In his report, Stuart said that while he did not want to subject Carlisle to a direct attack, his army needed rations, so he directed Fitzhugh Lee, one of his brigade commanders, to send in a flag of truce demanding unconditional surrender or bombardment.

Carlisle Barracks had its struggles in the aftermath of the fire. Post commander Captain Daniel Hastings issued a reported dated July 14, 1863, in which he described the damage:

> *On my return I found the buildings burned by the rebels. The brick walls are standing and many of them can be repaired and made available in reconstructing the Barracks. Two frame buildings are but slightly injured, one of which was used as a Quartermaster storehouse and the other for offices.*

In his report, Hastings estimated that it would cost $70,000 to put the garrison back in good condition. He asked his superiors for permission to

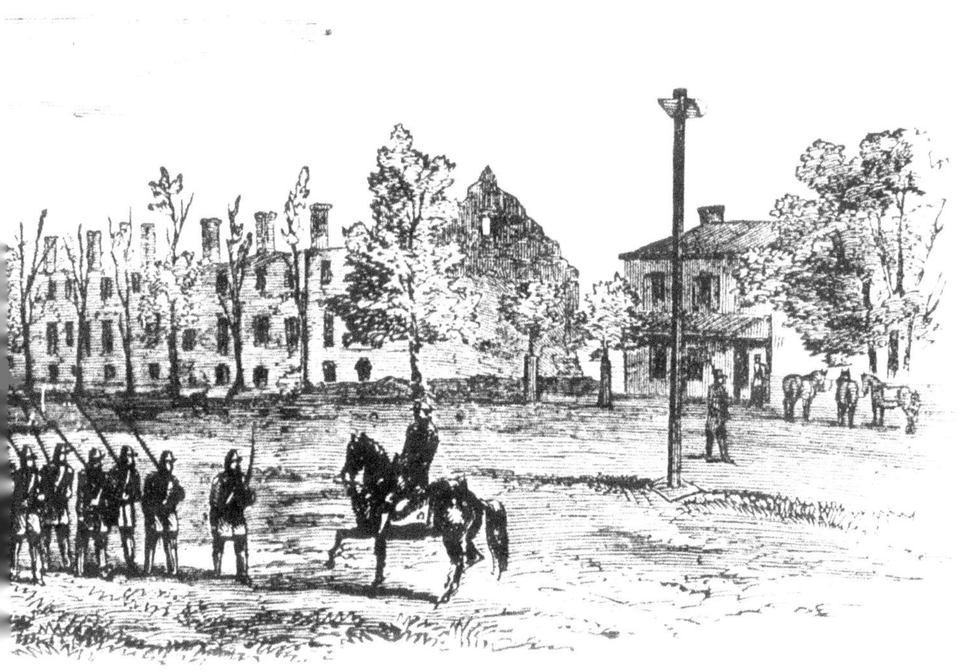

begin repairs as soon as possible to shelter men and horses before the onset of winter.

Brigadier General Montgomery Cunningham Meigs, the army quartermaster general, sent an architect to Carlisle to investigate conditions and make recommendations. That expert suggested that the army spend an estimated $23,200 to rebuild a row of officers' quarters, a barracks and a stable to shelter the men and horses on post.

The architect estimated that it would cost $47,600 to restore all of the buildings damaged in the fire. The strain of greater military priorities slowed repairs at Carlisle Barracks, so on September 20, Hastings wrote Meigs about the seriousness of the problem: "I have here nearly two hundred invalids and convalescents from the different cavalry regiments and no means of shelter other than a common tent."

This second appeal got results; shortly afterward, the quartermaster corps advertised for a large amount of yellow pine and hemlock lumber. The women of Carlisle responded to the commandant's call for help by bringing the sick and wounded warm clothes, food and delicacies. When the weather turned bitter cold, Carlisle residents loaned stoves to the post for soldiers' use. The first of the new buildings was completed by early November 1863.

"OUR LITTLE DIFFICULTY"

The Return of Fitzhugh Lee

It may just as well have been a force of nature. The *Evening Sentinel*, on February 28, 1896, described the crowd as a "veritable migration" to Carlisle Barracks, helped along by a cloudless sky and convenient trolley service.

> *Each car went "hanging full" to increase the throng gathered on the walks before the large gymnasium building. When at last the doors were thrown open for admission an animated scene ensued, for everyone in the crowd of many hundreds seemed bent upon entering the hall at the same moment, in defiance of the law of physics which says that "large bodies move slowly."*

It created quite a stir among Carlisle residents when Captain Richard Pratt, founder of the Carlisle Industrial Indian School, announced the guests for the annual commencement. An old enemy was invited to the ceremony to honor the seventeen boys and eight girls graduating from the school designed to assimilate native children into the white man's culture.

The event drew a crowd of about three thousand—the largest audience yet for an Indian School commencement. No doubt, some of it had to do with Fitzhugh Lee, a man both hated and loved in Carlisle depending on who you talked to. In a headline, *The Sentinel* announced, "The Citizens of Carlisle Extend a Universal and Most Hearty Welcome to Gen. Fitzhugh Lee."

That same day, however, the *Carlisle Daily Herald* quoted excerpts from Donavin's account of the shelling of Carlisle to remind readers of the events of July 1, 1863. In its editorial, the newspaper criticized the decision by Pratt to invite Lee to speak at commencement:

> *Many things in war and even in rebellion…can be overlooked, but firing upon women and children is not one of them. The laws of war condemn it. It was a disgrace to the Rebel uniform Fitzhugh Lee wore, to the State from which he hailed, to his manhood and to the name of Lee he bears that*

> *the women and children were fired upon by his command. It was a mistake to invite him…not because he was a Rebel but because he did a disgraceful and unsoldierly thing that cannot be justified.*

Partway through the ceremony, Pratt stepped forward and introduced Pennsylvania governor Daniel H. Hastings, son of the officer who commanded Carlisle Barracks when it was burned by Confederate troops. "General Lee was up here once before some years ago," Hastings said. "We gave him a warm welcome then, and we give him a warmer welcome now. We returned his call; he gave us a warm reception, and now we will give him another reception."

Pratt then introduced Lee—humorously referring to him as "the man who burned these buildings 30 years ago, so that they might be rebuilt in better shape." Lee responded by saying that the welcome from Carlisle "deeply touches my heart, because I believe it comes from your hearts." The general then recalled his past days on post as a young officer drilling recruits on the parade grounds. Lee explained how he was then ordered to Texas, where he became acquainted with the Indians—"the red rovers of the plains," as he put it—receiving as a memento a scar from an arrow wound inflicted by a Comanche warrior.

"I came past this town on my way to Gettysburg and asked the commander of Carlisle to surrender the place, which he refused to do," Lee told the audience.

> *What might have been the result of our little difficulty cannot be known, for the next morning, the order reached me to proceed to Gettysburg. But all this is past and I rejoice with you that there is rest on the sword. This is a great country and it is our chief duty to support this great flag of ours.*

Lee said that the South rejoiced in the peace and would be ready in the future to defend liberty.

The *Daily Herald* fired back on March 2 with an editorial defending its position. Quoting Lee, the newspaper argued that had it not been for the order to report to Gettysburg, Lee would have kept right on shelling Carlisle until Smith surrendered: "It is no wonder that through the audience of Carlisle people…were such comments as 'That man ought not to be here.' 'That man ought not to have been asked here.'"

In making its case against Lee, the *Daily Herald* cited William T. Sherman as an example of the proper way to conduct war, saying that the Union general had been justified in shelling Atlanta for its military targets and that Sherman had exercised restraint in halting the shelling of civilians in Columbia, South Carolina. Once again, the *Daily Herald* called on readers to condemn Lee and his visit: "As far as this paper is concerned, it will resent any injury to the people of Carlisle by him or any other unrepentant Rebel."

On February 29, the *Evening Sentinel* published an editorial comment from an unidentified writer condemning the *Carlisle Herald* editorial of the day before as an insult to an honored guest that was "universally" denounced by local residents. *The Sentinel* also ran an excerpt from the *Philadelphia Record* that described Lee as "the same man, grown older and wiser, and not afraid or ashamed to say so."

The night before commencement, on February 26, the Indian School hosted an assembly in which prominent educators and politicians spoke on the future of the American Indian. The *Evening Sentinel* reported how Lee spoke briefly, relating a humorous story about hazing at West Point.

It seemed some upperclassmen had ordered a first-year cadet from North Carolina to sing or make a speech. The plebe remarked how he had never made a speech in his life but thought he could sing "Down on the Tar River," if only he could get the right pitch. "I have got the pitch," General Lee said. "This school and the work of Captain Pratt had given it to me. I have faith in this work." Lee then cut himself short, joking about how he was invited to speak at commencement. "I have too great an appreciation of the compliment paid me by this audience…to inflict two speeches on you," *The Sentinel* quoted him as saying.

Another guest of Pratt was Union general Oliver O. Howard, a former rival of Fitzhugh Lee on the battlefield, who spoke on February 28 at an event hosted by the Captain Colwell Post No. 201 of the Grand Army of the Republic. *The Sentinel* reported that Howard was introduced by Brigadier General Robert M. Henderson, a local judge, who spoke briefly about how Howard and Lee reconciled and shook hands during the commencement ceremony.

> *We are proud of them both—the blue and the gray. What was the war worth? It was fruitless if it did not bring all the people of these two great sections together in love. Without that the war was a failure and this peace a curse.*

Both Howard and Lee toured the Gettysburg battlefield with prominent Carlisle residents. Reports were that the former enemies rode in the same carriage and on the same seat, talking freely of the epic battle. "Neither at Carlisle nor at Gettysburg was there an incident to interrupt the scene of

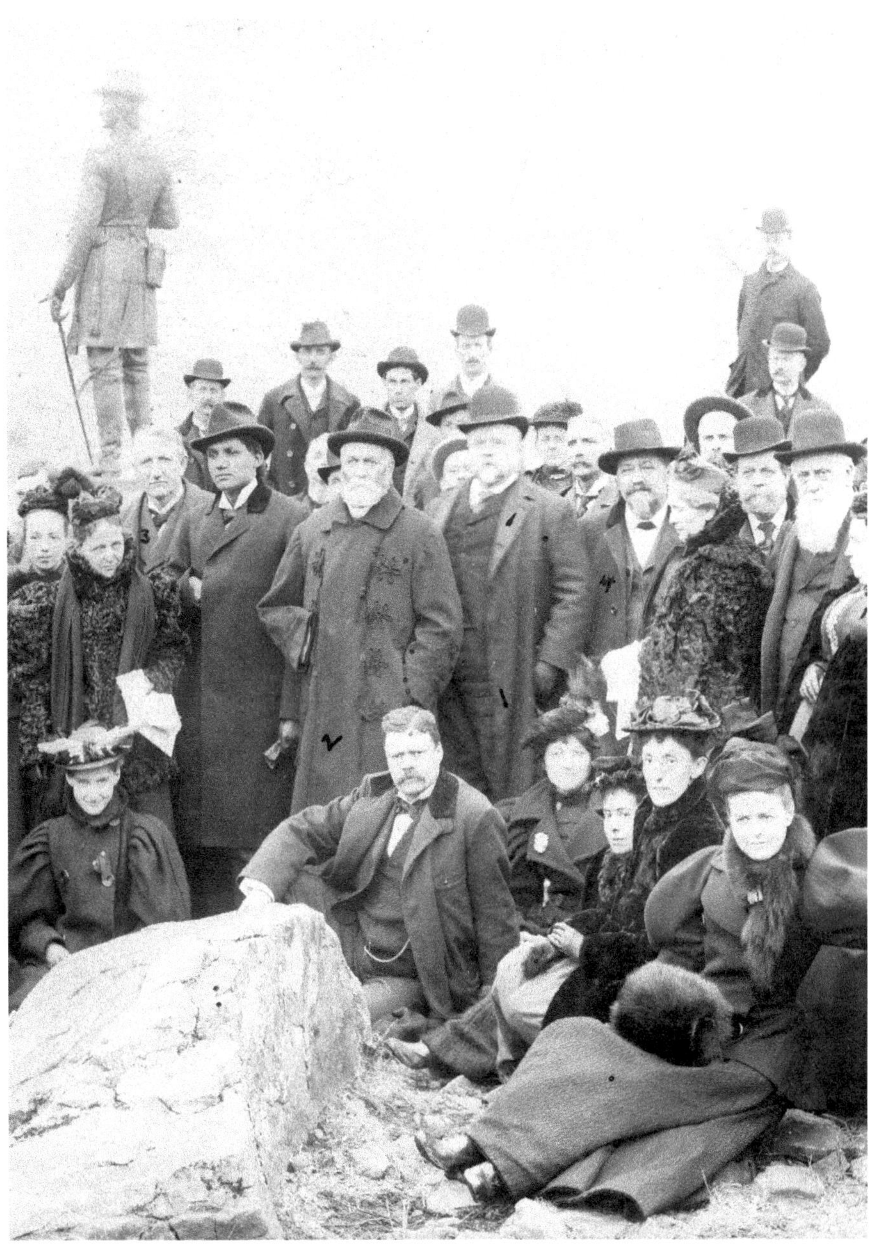

This group photograph at the Gettysburg Battlefield was taken on General Lee's first return visit to Carlisle. Numbered are: 1. Fitzhugh Lee; 2. General O.O. Howard; 3. Captain Richard H. Pratt; and 4. Captain William Miller, a Medal of Honor winner from Carlisle. *Courtesy of CCHS.*

unity and concord between representatives of the once divided sections," *The Sentinel* reported in its February 29 edition.

"It was a sight that must have brought tears to the eyes of the angels of peace to see those two warriors on the field of Gettysburg," Henderson said in his introduction. During his speech, Howard expressed pleasure at meeting the people of Carlisle, along with his belief that Fitzhugh Lee was a good man.

"I suppose he did some mischief when he shelled Carlisle, but you must remember that it was the fate of war," Howard said. "We shelled Vicksburg, Richmond, Columbia and other cities and towns for our southern friends. Let's have no more of war." Howard added that, given the circumstances, it would probably have been better for Union general William Smith to have evacuated the town and have it out with Lee on open ground.

The commencement was not the first time Lee tried to explain his actions. On August 25, 1882, Lee wrote a letter to Jacob T. Zug, secretary of the Carlisle Manufacturing Company, in which he tried to set the record straight on why his men may have burned down the lumberyard owned by a friend of Zug's. Based on a description of the scope and location of the business, Lee believed that his men may have thought the lumberyard was either public or government owned, "but I cannot give a certificate to that effect…I do not recollect nor can I recall the circumstances."

He reminded Zug that his uncle, Robert E. Lee, had strict orders against the destruction of private property while the Confederate army was in Pennsylvania. Fitzhugh Lee was convinced that no man in his command would so flagrantly disobey orders because his sense of duty would not permit it. Fitzhugh Lee did confirm that his troops were in Carlisle.

When Smith refused to surrender, there was nothing left to do but to fight for Carlisle, Fitzhugh Lee wrote.

> *When that alternative was presented, I sent a staff officer to General Smith telling him I was going to attack, but would wait for him to put the women and children in places of safety…It was with much regret I proceeded with hostile intent against Carlisle. Some of the most pleasant days of my life were passed in the hospitable homes of her people.*

An article published in a local newspaper described how the death of Fitzhugh Lee on April 28, 1905, stirred up memories among old-timers. It made specific reference to the shelling as "an effectual way of impressing his name upon their memories, but a very bad way to win their love and respect."

The article reminded readers that "that was in a time of war" and that Lee once was a young army lieutenant stationed at Carlisle Barracks,

> *well acquainted with many of the best families of the town. He was handsome in person, dignified in bearing, courteous and very popular. He figured at many of our social affairs and also participated in the sports of the day.*

One resident related how Lee took "a keen interest in chicken fights [and dog fights] horses and kindred frolics." The article mentions how Colonel Charles May, barracks commander at the time, had a champion dog that could defeat any dog in Carlisle and vicinity. Lee learned of a champion dog in Mechanicsburg and managed to borrow it long enough to "give May's dog a good licking which pleased Lee but made May very mad."

While at Carlisle Barracks, Lee befriended Lieutenant William Woods Averill, whom he later fought against during the Civil War when Averill was colonel of the Third Pennsylvania Cavalry. When soldiers under Lee captured a captain under Averill, he treated that officer with "marked civility" and even took him to the theatre one night.

ENDURING LEGACY

Up until now, *Remembering Carlisle* has been about events, people and places that have come and gone. This final chapter will focus on the origins of local institutions that carry over into today. It starts with three places of learning that continue to have an impact on current generations. It goes on to describe a legendary athlete whose fame persists as the Jim Thorpe Sports Days, an annual competition among war colleges held every year at Carlisle Barracks. Lastly, there is the story of how two friends set in motion the car show phenomena that has put Carlisle on the map.

"A Well Cultivated Mind"

Dickinson College and Dickinson School of Law

By his own admission, future president James Buchanan was a wild child prone to peer pressure in a college town full of distractions. Buchanan studied hard when he first arrived in Carlisle in September 1807. He was driven by family obligations to apply himself at Dickinson College with the goal of graduating with honors before taking on an apprenticeship in a law office. It was thought that the young Buchanan could go into real estate to support his family back in Mercersburg.

As a young boy of sixteen, he had no trouble keeping up with assignments in Latin, Greek, philosophy, math, literature, geography, logic and history. Viewed as stuffy, Buchanan was teased by classmates, prompting him to pursue more extracurricular activities. "Chiefly from the example of others, and in order to be considered a clever and spirited youth, I engaged in every sort of extravagance and mischief," he later wrote.

His drinking became disruptive and got the attention of faculty. He smoked cigars in defiance of college regulations. But worst of all, Buchanan was conceited and arrogant to his professors. Despite distractions, Buchanan kept up with his class work and ended his first year at Dickinson with an excellent academic record. Confident, the future commander in chief was shocked when a letter arrived home advising him that he was being expelled from college due to his disorderly conduct.

Buchanan turned to his pastor, Dr. John King, president of the college board of trustees. It was King who had urged the Buchanan family to enroll James at Dickinson. King saw potential in the boy's keen mind, along with the opportunity to recruit a student to help revive sagging enrollment. King made Buchanan swear to behave during his second year at Dickinson. The young man followed through and graduated, eventually becoming the fifteenth U.S. president. He remains the highest-ranking and perhaps the most famous Dickinson College alumnus.

Dickinson College had its origins in a frontier grammar school established in 1773 on the south side of Liberty Alley, just west of Bedford Street. In 1781, the school oversight committee asked the presbytery to take the school under its care and have it chartered as an academy.

Hearing this, Dr. Benjamin Rush of Philadelphia was interested in the project but favored a college instead of an academy. He received help from Colonel John Montgomery of Carlisle—one of the men who patented the grammar school. What Montgomery lacked in formal education, he made up for in civil service as an associate justice, town burgess and justice of the peace.

First, the two friends had to sell the idea to influential members of the First Presbyterian Church on the square. On September 3, 1782, Rush issued a paper entitled "Hints for Establishing a College at Carlisle." He said that the town could serve as a central location to draw young Presbyterians together

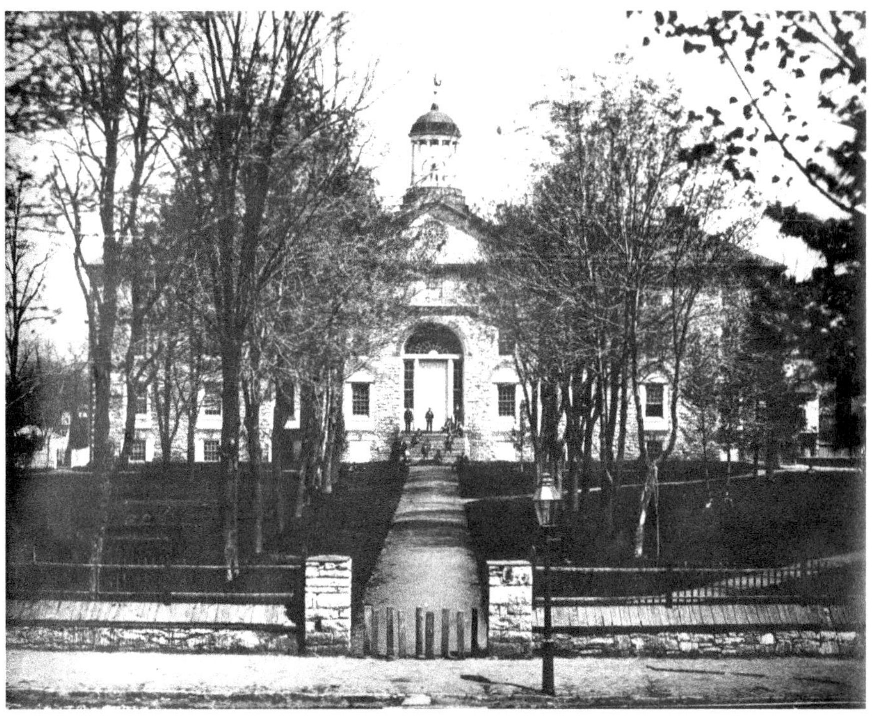

This photograph of Old West at Dickinson College was taken circa 1870. *Courtesy of CCHS.*

for a cheaper education than in any other Pennsylvania village in "one of the most healthy spots in the state."

During a speech made at the centennial commencement in 1883, college president Dr. George Crooks recalled the enthusiasm that Rush brought to the process: "What buoyant hopes were his. What unwavering love for the child of his affection." The incessant lobbying by Rush had the desired effect. On September 9, 1783, the state assembly passed a resolution establishing a college named for John Dickinson, president of the supreme executive council. Dickinson had the following to say during an organizational meeting held on April 6, 1784, at the county courthouse in Carlisle:

> *When the inhabitants of this and neighboring counties observe your faithful labors for communicating to their youth the resources of science collected by the wise and good of all nations, what father can be so cruel as not to strive that his child shall partake of the distribution. Miserably,*

will he deceive himself by supposing any inheritance he can bequeath is to be compared to a well cultivated mind.

During the meeting, organizers voted unanimously to elect Dr. Charles Nisbet principal of the college. Rush sent letters to persuade Nisbet to make the overseas voyage from Scotland to a fresh opportunity in Carlisle. Indeed, Nisbet was in for a warm reception of fever and chills when he arrived in Carlisle on July 4, 1785.

Thirty women and forty men rode out to Boiling Springs and then to the Carlisle Iron Works to greet Nisbet and his family. There they dined together before the entourage rode into Carlisle, where bells rang and a welcoming crowd had gathered. The following day, professors and students marched in procession to First Presbyterian Church, where Nisbet took the oath of office and delivered an inaugural sermon.

The doctor and his family soon contracted malaria after they were quartered at the abandoned Carlisle Barracks on government land surrounded by swamp. Within weeks of their arrival, Nisbet complained about how the "sickly and dirty town of Carlisle" led to suffering so protracted that he became unfit for work. At first, he attributed the sickness to the intense heat and unfavorable climate.

Nisbet wrote to friends about being deceived about the quality of the town and about the enrollment and fiscal condition of the college. He learned of a proposal by the trustees to reduce his annual salary due to revenue shortfalls from £250 British sterling to £300 in Pennsylvania currency.

Nisbet submitted his resignation on October 19, 1785. But the onset of cold weather not only delayed his voyage back to Scotland until spring but also cured him of his illness. Nisbet submitted a letter requesting reinstatement to General John Armstrong of Carlisle, acting president of the board of trustees:

Having now by the Divine Goodness recovered my health and retaining the same affection to this country which led me to abandon my native soil. I beg the favor that you would communicate to the trustees this unexpected change in my situation.

In the end, Nisbet stayed on as president until 1804, when he died. Dickinson College operated out of the grammar school until 1805, when it moved to its present location on the west side of Carlisle. Back then, students had to be fourteen years old to be enrolled and had to pay only forty-four dollars for tuition, room and board and other costs.

Though separate institutions, Dickinson College and Dickinson School of Law share a common name and heritage. The origin of the state's oldest law school came out of a letter that Judge John Reed wrote to the college board of trustees in June 1833. The son of a Revolutionary War general, Reed graduated from Dickinson College before studying law under the tutelage of a Gettysburg attorney. In 1809, he started his own practice in Westmoreland County and, three years later, became a state deputy attorney general.

In July 1820, Reed became president judge of the Ninth Judicial District, which included parts of what are now Cumberland, Franklin, Perry and Adams Counties. Reed moved to Carlisle and lived here for twelve years before buying the lot on the southwest corner of West High and South West Streets. On this lot, Reed built the home that he occupied until his death in 1850. The first version of the law school operated out of this building, now the home of the Dickinson College president.

Reed only wanted his law school to be affiliated in name to the college. He would shoulder the financial burden related to operating the school as a professor of law. The trustees granted his request on September 27, 1833, and officially approved the plan on January 9, 1834. The judge advertised his school in the eleven editions of the *American Volunteer*, a local newspaper, leading up to the April 1, 1834 start date.

Back then, tuition was seventy-five dollars a year, and the program could be completed in two years if the student had prior college or was properly prepared. Thirty-five students graduated from "Judge Reed's Law School" from 1834 to 1850, including Andrew Curtin, Pennsylvania governor during the Civil War.

Upon his death, Reed left no mechanism behind to continue the law school, so it remained dormant until 1862, when the college appointed Judge James Graham as professor of law. Like Reed, Graham had local ties. He was born in West Pennsboro Township, Cumberland County, and graduated from Dickinson College in 1827. Graham ran the program until the fall of 1882, when he died, ending the second phase of the law school.

Eight years would pass before Dickinson School of Law was reorganized as an independent nonprofit corporation separate from Dickinson College. In earlier years, the line between the two institutions was harder to distinguish. Law school courses were included in the college catalogue as though it was simply a department of the college. Law school students often participated in college activities and played on its athletic teams. Both institutions held identical graduation exercises.

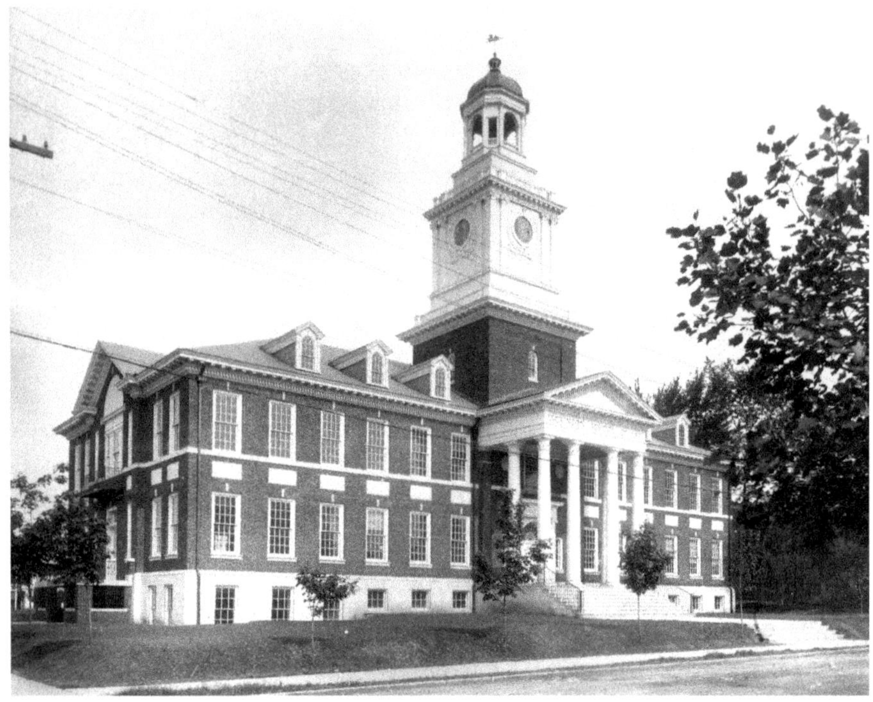

This photograph of Trickett Hall at Dickinson School of Law was taken circa 1918. *Courtesy of CCHS.*

Close friends Wilbur Fisk Sadler and William Trickett were involved in this critical stage of the law school's development. Sadler directed the 1890 reorganization effort, while Trickett would serve as its first dean for thirty-eight years. During his tenure, the campus moved in 1917 from Emory Hall at West and Pomfret Streets to the main academic building on South College Street known to locals as Trickett Hall.

Sadler and Trickett knew each other for years before the reorganization. A preacher, Trickett had left the ministry and entered Dickinson College in 1866—one year after Sadler, an attorney, was admitted to the Cumberland County Bar. Trickett had turned to Sadler for legal advice in June 1874, when he was dismissed as a professor from Dickinson College due to a disagreement over policy.

In discussing the case, Sadler noticed that Trickett had a flair for legal matters, so he persuaded his friend to study law. Trickett took up the challenge and was admitted to the bar a year later, on August 26, 1875. The idea of reviving the law school gathered momentum at a meeting of the college trustees on January 9, 1890.

Dickinson School of Law was independent for over a century, until July 1997, when it officially became part of Pennsylvania State University. Six years later, in November 2003, an anonymous source leaked a confidential memo to *The Sentinel* revealing a proposal to forsake Carlisle and relocate Dickinson School of Law to University Park.

This caused such a public uproar that Penn State ultimately agreed to develop a dual law school campus in Carlisle and State College. Trickett Hall was in the process of being renovated and expanded during the writing of this book. The Carlisle campus is set to reopen at the Trickett Hall location in January 2010.

"They...Give Themselves Up to Learning"

The Carlisle Indian School

Luther Standing Bear fought like a brave just to reach his father. The Indian chief was surrounded by a crowd of boys, all vying to shake his hand. "Everybody ran downstairs to see my father," Luther later wrote. "There were several tribes at the school. Many of whom heard of father. They were anxious to see him."

Standing Bear looked distinguished enough as the center of attention—all dapper in a gray suit, nice shoes and a derby. He even sported a gold watch and chain but still wore his hair long in the tradition of the Sioux. As they reunited, Luther Standing Bear could not officially talk to his father. The rules were clear: students of the Carlisle Industrial Indian School could only talk in English.

The trouble was that the Indian chief could not speak the language of the white man. There must have been an awkward silence as father and son greeted each other, until Luther wrote a note to the school superintendent, Richard Pratt, asking for permission to speak in Sioux. To his son, Standing Bear spoke of a painful reality and of hope for the future:

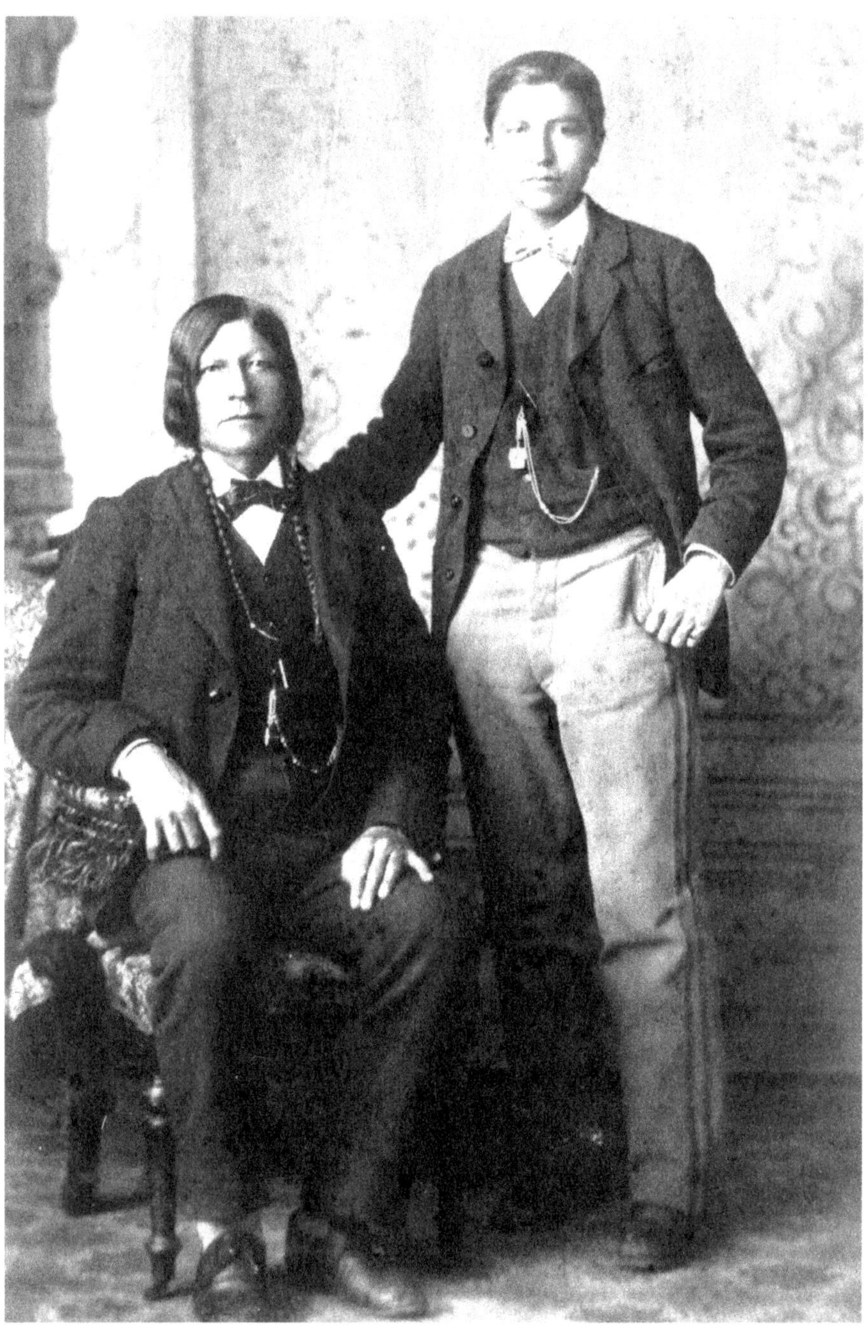

Luther Standing Bear stands beside his father, Standing Bear, in this cabinet card photo by John N. Choate, circa 1881. *Courtesy of CCHS.*

Enduring Legacy

There is nothing but the Long Knives everywhere I went, and they keep coming like flies. So we all have to learn their ways, in order that we may be able to live with them. You will have to learn all you can, and I will see that your brothers and sisters follow in the path you are making for them.

For Luther, the path began with a long train ride from Springfield, Dakota, in the fall of 1879. He was among the first enrolled in a social experiment to assimilate native boys and girls into the white man's culture. Everywhere the children went, people came out at all hours to watch them pass on their way east to Carlisle Barracks. A crowd of hundreds had gathered at the train station when the first students pulled into town about midnight on October 6.

Wrapped tightly in blankets, the children were escorted to the open gates of an army post that had stood abandoned for seven years. There, they were split up by gender and given instructions. "They told us to go to a certain building and pointed it out to us," Luther wrote. "We ran very fast, expecting to find nice little beds like those the white people had. We were so tired and worn out from the long trip. We wanted a good long sleep."

Instead, the boys found nothing but bare floor to sleep on. They could hear the girls cry out in the early morning hours, cold, tired and lonely. So began the dream of Pratt, who thought of Indians as human beings, not as savages.

A veteran soldier, Pratt deeply believed that the best way to civilize the Indian was to bring him into civilization and invite him to stay. He felt that the best solution was to take Indians away from tribal influences and put them among the white man to learn a useful trade. Pratt first put this thinking into practice as the jailer of violent Indians rounded up on the western frontier and imprisoned in Florida.

Pratt removed their chains and put the natives to work making souvenirs to sell to tourists. He allowed them to keep the money they earned. From their number, he selected the most trustworthy to guard fellow Indians, and at his encouragement, they learned how to work in the mills and farms. Many converted to Christianity and took to wearing white man's clothes as they learned the English language.

Very soon, Pratt and his inmates began to realize that the best chance of success was to train young Indians not yet set in their native ways. But resources in Florida were limited for Pratt to realize his dream of establishing a school for Indian children in the east. Pratt decided that Carlisle Barracks

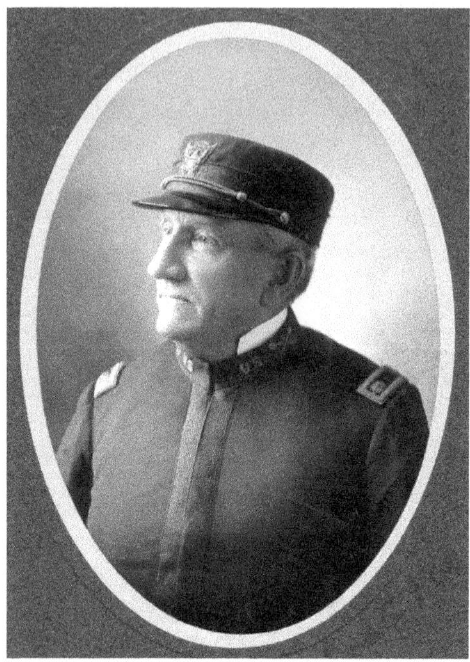

This photograph of Captain Richard Pratt was taken circa 1900, while he was still superintendent of the Carlisle Industrial Indian School. *Courtesy of CCHS.*

was the ideal location, so he lobbied the Department of the Interior to get the post on loan from the War Department. The army closed Carlisle Barracks in 1871 due to its small size and the poor relations the garrison had with local residents.

Merchants missed the money that soldiers used to spend in town. When Pratt visited Carlisle to explain his vision, he left with a long list of supporters who signed a petition encouraging the federal government to establish an Indian school on post. Pratt was successful in securing government approval but had to convince tribal leaders like Spotted Tail, who questioned his motives.

"White people are thieves and liars. We do not want our children to learn such things," Spotted Tail told Pratt. But Standing Bear agreed with Pratt that the best way to avoid the abuses of the past was to learn the white man's culture and language.

In his writings, Luther recalled the day he received his name from Indian School staff. Students were told that the strange markings on the blackboard were the names of white men. The teacher instructed each boy to pick any name he wanted using a long, pointed stick. Each time a name was picked, it was written on a piece of tape, and the letters were erased from the blackboard. The teacher then stuck the tape on each boy's shirt.

"None of the names were read or explained to us so of course we did not know the sound or meaning of any of them," Luther recalled. "I took the pointer and acted as if I were about to touch an enemy…Soon we all had names of white men sewed on our backs."

The first time the teacher called roll, no one answered to his given name. One at a time, she had each boy stand and say "present" until they could associate the sound of the name with the identity of the student. Luther picked up on this fairly quickly. He scratched his name so deeply into the slate, he was never able to fully erase it. One time, he took a piece of chalk and wrote "Luther" over every possible surface in his living quarters just for the practice.

Pratt believed that without knowledge of English, the Indian was left helpless in any situation requiring communication with the white man. The teaching of language was so important to Pratt that he soon dismissed all of the interpreters and insisted that only English be spoken on campus. Pratt was proud of the progress his students made after only a few months of instruction. He wrote to a congressman that their eagerness to learn was the same as the average white student:

> *They have yielded gracefully to discipline...Isolated, as these Indian youth are from the savage surroundings at their homes, they lose that tenacity to the savage life which is so much an obstacle to Agency efforts and give themselves up to learning all they can in the time they expect to remain here.*

Pratt wrote his letter in January 1880, two months after the school had officially opened. At first, it was poorly funded by the U.S. government and survived only on donations from such groups as the Society of Friends. In those early days, older Indian boys learned enough carpentry skills to repair barracks buildings and convert a large stable into a workshop for instruction in the trades. With government support, the Indian school became more self-sufficient, with students growing the food used on campus and providing upkeep and services through the trades.

Pratt took Indian education one step further when he initiated the Outing system in 1880. Under this, boys and girls who qualified were sent out into the country to work for families. They were paid for the various duties they performed. Local families liked the idea because it gave them an extra pair of hands when labor was still very manual. The Indian children ate, lived and worked with their host family as they saved money and wrote letters home.

At its height, the Carlisle Indian school flourished to nearly one thousand students, and its athletic teams competed against America's leading universities. Indian School graduates entered a variety of professions, including government, medicine and law. The Indian School operated for thirty-nine years before it was closed in 1918.

A small graveyard with almost two hundred students sits just off the Claremont Road entrance to Carlisle Barracks. Today, the Cumberland County Historical Society receives inquiries from around the world from people seeking to trace their ancestral roots through the school.

"A BURST OF TRIUMPH"

Jim Thorpe and Carlisle

They were there to lead the Bright Path through the streets of Carlisle Town. A team of Indian School students, wearing nightshirts and white caps, pulled the carriage of Olympic heroes to the Elks Clubhouse. Standing by watching, an *Evening Sentinel* reporter was drawn to the action:

> *As the boys paraded, they gave snake dances amid the glare of red and yellow light, creating a scene somewhat beautiful, and slightly weird, but surely noisy. The red skins let out some pretty blood-curdling yells, and at once proved that their ability was inherited.*

There were admirers everywhere that Jim Thorpe went on August 16, 1912. The whole town celebrated the return of the rare and wonderful athlete who had won gold in both the pentathlon and decathlon. Dinner at the Elks was just the nightcap of a whirlwind day of activity—not just for Thorpe, but also for his legendary coach, Glen "Pop" Warner, and Louis Tewanima, a fellow Indian School student who had won the silver in the ten-thousand-meter race at Stockholm, Sweden.

The *Evening Herald* reported that ten thousand people lined West High Street to witness the parade of marching bands, fire companies, Indian School students and dignitaries. It started out from the square as the town clock struck 2:00 p.m. "Crowds cheered as the procession moved by, handkerchiefs were waving and colors flying everywhere. It was a burst of triumph," the reporter wrote.

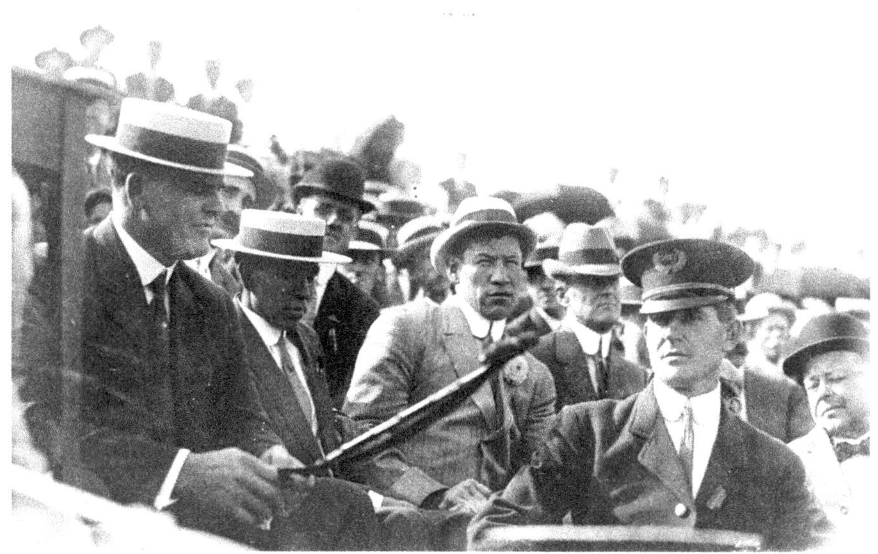

Pop Warner, Lewis Tewanima and Jim Thorpe sit in the grandstand at Biddle Field during the celebration following the 1912 Olympics. *Courtesy of CCHS.*

Five thousand people gathered at Biddle Field on the campus of Dickinson College to honor the three men. *The Sentinel* reported that the Indian School superintendent had special words for Thorpe: "You have covered yourself with glory. By your achievement, you have immeasurably helped your own race. By your victory, you have inspired your people to live a cleaner, healthier and more vigorous life."

When called to speak, Thorpe summed up his feelings: "You have shown us a splendid time, and we are grateful for it." Indeed, it was only the start of a day that featured fireworks, a formal dance, band concerts and a nightshirt parade. No one, least of all Thorpe, suspected his looming downfall.

A native of Oklahoma, Thorpe was given the name *Wa-Tho-Huck*, or "Bright Path," by his mother, a granddaughter of Black Hawk, chief of the Sac and Fox Indians. The story goes that she looked out the window of their one-room cabin and noticed how the sun lit a path to the door.

As Thorpe grew up, he took to running, jumping, swimming, wrestling, riding and climbing. Hunting and fishing were part of his childhood, along with helping with the chores. It was an agent of the Indian School in Carlisle who sold him on learning a trade. He came to town in 1904—a skinny boy of sixteen.

The Indian School had an extensive intramural program with trade shops forming teams. Thorpe played on the tailors' football team but drew little attention. Then came the day in the spring of 1907 when Warner first realized the athletic potential of Thorpe.

Thorpe was on cleanup detail after track practice when he noticed how all of the high jumpers failed to clear the bar at five feet, nine inches. When Thorpe asked if he could try, the jumpers snickered at the request because he was wearing overalls and had not warmed up. Thorpe cleared the bar with room to spare. Warner witnessed this feat and took to training Thorpe, who became a star not only in track and field but also in varsity football.

In 1911, Thorpe kicked four field goals and scored on a seventy-yard run to singlehandedly defeat Harvard 18–15. The following year, Thorpe scored twenty-two of the twenty-seven points against Army, including a touchdown that covered almost two hundred yards. He ran ninety-two yards for the score, only to have the play called back due to a rule infraction. He then ran ninety-seven yards on the very next play to score the touchdown.

The combination of Olympic gold and being named a first team all-American in football made 1912 the pivotal year for Thorpe. His was a household name, especially in Carlisle, where Thorpe was active in the community. He was a member of the Catholic youth group at the Indian School. Every Sunday, the group marched from the barracks to St. Patrick's Church on East Pomfret Street. Thorpe once played Santa Claus on Christmas night for about 275 Catholic students. He met his first wife, Iva Miller, through the group, and they were married in 1913.

Local reporter Arthur Martin, who covered the wedding, once served as a secretary to Warner. In a 1968 interview with the *Carlisle Shopper's Guide*, Martin said that Thorpe was lazy:

> *He wouldn't exert himself until he was behind, then he worked like Hell. I recall that many times Pop booted him in the rear end...Everybody was Thorpe's friend. He was so easy going. Everybody just wanted to be associated with him.*

The same *Shopper's Guide* story quoted Mrs. Edward L. Whisler, who taught voice and piano at the Indian School after Thorpe had left. "Jim had an open face," she said, "an honest look...eyes wide apart, a picture of frankness but not of brilliance. He would trust anybody."

Richard Kaseeta of Carlisle was an orphan when he came to the Indian School in 1907 at age four. "I called Thorpe 'Uncle Jim.' He used to carry me around on his shoulders."

Kaseeta believed that Thorpe was born fifty years too early for sports to provide him an affordable living. "In those days, sports were played more or less for the fun of the game, and the only big money was in the fight racket," Kaseeta said. "Today, all sports are big business…Thorpe could have gone into anything and…had all kinds of contracts and trophies thrown at him."

Kaseeta had watched Thorpe play football. "Jim was an explosive type. If a ball was handed to him, he was gone. He would hit like a freight train…He was a natural." Thorpe would sometimes visit Kaseeta, who worked summers for farm families. "Jim would go off by himself, select a distance the length of the pitcher from home plate and hurl walnuts through a knothole."

Baseball would come back to hurt Thorpe. Seven months after winning gold in Stockholm, the story broke that Thorpe had spent two seasons playing minor league ball in North Carolina and Arkansas. The Olympic committee had strict rules that banned professional athletes from Olympic competition.

Thorpe apologized, saying that he had only played for the love of the game and had received very little money. He was forced to return his medals and had his name removed from the record books. The medals were only restored to the Thorpe family in 1983—thirty years after Jim's death.

The loss haunted Thorpe for the rest of his life. He went on to play both professional baseball and football and was even elected president of the American Professional Football Association, forerunner of the National Football League. In early 1950, the Associated Press selected Thorpe for the twin honors of the greatest football player and outstanding male athlete of the half century. Again, Carlisle honored him.

The Sentinel reported that, in January 1950, Thorpe visited workers at the Carlisle Tire and Rubber plant and autographed large numbers of baseballs before eating lunch with the Rotary Club at the Molly Pitcher Hotel. He encouraged local residents to lobby Warner Brothers studio to have Carlisle host the world premiere of his biopic *Jim Thorpe—All American*.

Over fifteen thousand people attended a tribute to Thorpe held in August 1951 to celebrate the movie premiere and the dedication of a historic marker in the Veterans Memorial Courtyard on the square. But not all was right with Thorpe. He had developed an alcohol habit, and his bouts with drinking were plentiful.

In his later years, Thorpe traveled across the country in search of steady money. His jobs included being a guard at an auto plant, a superintendent of recreation in the Chicago park system and bit parts in movies. He toured the nation, speaking about his life and experiences while dressed in full Indian regalia.

Thorpe died of a heart attack on March 28, 1953. At one point, Carlisle was considered a possible burial place for Thorpe because it was here where he had first achieved fame. A committee of local residents even had a grave site picked out near the field where Thorpe used to play football. The effort failed, and instead Thorpe's third wife made burial arrangements with two towns in northeast Pennsylvania that had no previous ties to her husband. "Pat just wanted too much money for the body," John B. Fowler, a Carlisle civic leader told *Sports Illustrated* in 1983.

In 1957, citizens of Mauch Chunk and East Mauch Chunk approved a referendum unifying their two towns under the new name of Jim Thorpe. The hope was that the tomb could draw tourism to the two towns, which, at the time, were suffering from economic woes.

"THE REST IS HISTORY"

The First Carlisle Car Show

Foot by foot...yard by yard...the two men worked in pursuit of a dream. Elliott "Chip" Miller and Bill Miller Jr., though not related, may as well have been brothers. For days on end, they had worked from dawn until dusk mapping out Carlisle Fairgrounds into a grid pattern.

Postwar '74 was just around the corner. The two friends were running out of time. They had to hurry if they wanted to plot out six hundred vendor spaces before the event. "We had to measure the whole fairgrounds with a three-hundred-foot tape measure," Bill Jr. said. "We took our vacations to lay out the field. That was the old days."

The Millers were fortunate that Chip had a mechanical drawing background. This made it easier to prepare the grid for the first Carlisle

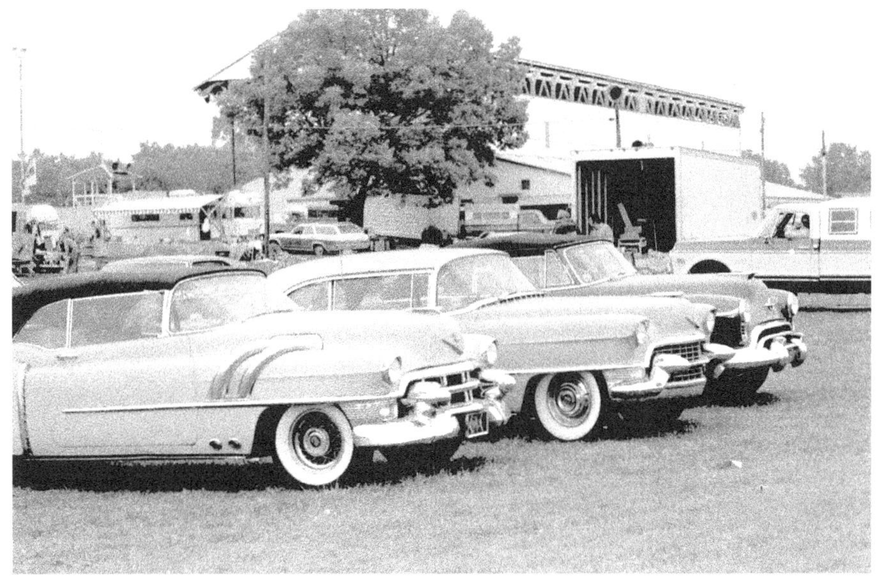

This photograph of Postwar '74 was taken by a *Sentinel* photographer on September 26, 1974. The fairgrounds grandstand is in the background. *Courtesy of CCHS.*

car show held from September 26 to 29, 1974. Back then, they used paper plates held down by gutter spikes to designate each space, but Mother Nature caused a problem.

"We wrote on each plate what the space number was," Bill Jr. recalled. "Well, it rained and everything got messed up. We were not finished until the day of the event. We started this as a fun thing to do to show cars of the era we enjoyed. That is what it started out to be."

The two men first met in 1969 and instantly became close friends. They shared a passion for cars and regularly attended events, including the antique auto show held each year in Hershey. During the 1973 show, the Millers were asked to bring a car to the Milestone Car Society booth to draw attention to what was then a fledgling club forming in Pennsylvania. Now, Milestone is a national organization.

Chip owned a 1954 Corvette that he wanted to sell, so it seemed the perfect opportunity. But event officials told the Millers that the car was not old enough to sell, and they had to remove it from the grounds. It shocked them to learn that a car had to have been made prior to 1939 to qualify. Both men were only in their twenties and had a hard time relating to cars made before they were born. As Hershey was their favorite show, they were disappointed that they could not participate with what they considered to be an old car.

As they removed the Corvette, Chip said that it was a shame there was no venue to showcase late-model cars. Bill Jr. agreed and suggested that they do something about it. The more they talked, the more excited they got over the prospect of putting on their own show. They each invested $500 and formed a company called Postwar Events to promote a show for enthusiasts of cars made after World War II.

The friends then had to book a venue. They looked at the York Fairgrounds, Williams Grove Speedway, the Pennsylvania Farm Show complex and Willow Mill amusement park. "We had no idea what size it was going to be," Bill Jr. recalled. "We chose Carlisle because we thought it was the most convenient location."

Three major highways intersect in Carlisle, creating a strategic transportation hub—what Bill Jr. calls "the keystone of the Keystone State." The Pennsylvania Turnpike, Interstate 81 and Route 11 make access to car show events relatively easy. He added that the coming together of three highways is the major reason Carlisle attracts trucking and distribution firms. Early on, the Millers decided to hold their event the week before the Hershey show. They figured that car enthusiasts coming to their show could then go to Hershey.

The first Carlisle car show had its share of challenges. Both men had full-time jobs—Bill Jr. at a car dealership and Chip selling conveyers. They had no experience putting on a show. "We didn't have a clue what we were doing…It was all fresh to us," Bill Jr. said. "We had to learn as we went."

Starting in May 1974, the Millers went to car shows almost every weekend to pass out fliers promoting their event and to invite vendors to Postwar '74. They also advertised in trade journals and car hobby magazines. About six hundred vendors signed on that first year.

Locally, the Millers enlisted the help of the Cumberland County Tourist Council to help promote the event. The council knew that the show was going to bring people into the area. "Don Haywood, owner of the Embers Motel, was council president and helped us with our mailings," Bill Jr. said. "He was very instrumental in making the early days as smooth as possible for us so we could get the show publicized."

Information packets were sent out to vendors with details on everything from the swap meet to local motels and restaurants. The council also set up a booth at Postwar '74 to welcome guests and to supply them with information on the area. Since other car shows were done by nonprofit organizations offering free admission, the Millers had to be careful about pricing their commercial show. The first year, they charged a one-dollar admission, while children under twelve were admitted free.

The Millers had their doubtful moments. A month before the event, they were sitting in a café in York trying to decide whether to cancel Postwar '74. The situation was bleak in the midst of the energy crisis, which called to question the practicality of a car show.

"You couldn't get gas," Bill Jr. recalled. "There were long lines everywhere. The gas stations would only be open an hour in the morning." The crisis created another concern. Big cars were not selling because people were buying smaller vehicles with better gas mileage.

By that time, the Millers only had $300 of their initial $1,000 investment left to promote the event. Many people said that they couldn't attend because of the energy crisis. "It was really scaring everybody," Bill Jr. said. "They did not know what was going to happen, but we figured we came this far, we may as well keep right on doing it."

The weather cooperated, and six thousand people attended the first car show. The Millers were able to pay the $600 that the Carlisle fair association had charged for rent. By 1975, no one called the event "Postwar." It simply became known as "Carlisle." That year, it rained every day, creating a quagmire of mud for vendors and their vehicles.

"It was a nightmare," Bill Jr. said. "Tractor trailers sank down to the axles. There was no roadway. Farmers came from all over the place to try and get them out."

Not only did this destroy the fairground turf, but it also tracked mud throughout Carlisle. A friend named Paul Snyder helped the Millers to restore the show field at a cost of $1,000. The year 1977 saw similar problems for the fall show but also debuted Spring Carlisle and the first ever car corral, a used car lot for collector cars.

The rent increased every year in response to "heat" association members were receiving from municipal officials concerned about the influx of thousands of people to the shows. By 1981, the rent hit $15,000, and Bill Jr. joked, "For that kind of money, you ought to sell us the place." The association took him seriously, sending them a sales agreement that advised the Millers they had thirty days to accept the offer.

"With interest rates at 20 percent, it was pretty interesting when we tried to finance the fairgrounds," Bill Jr. said. "We eventually ended up at Farmers Trust Company." It turned out that Hayward was on the bank's board of directors, and Snyder had controlling interest in the fairgrounds. That helped

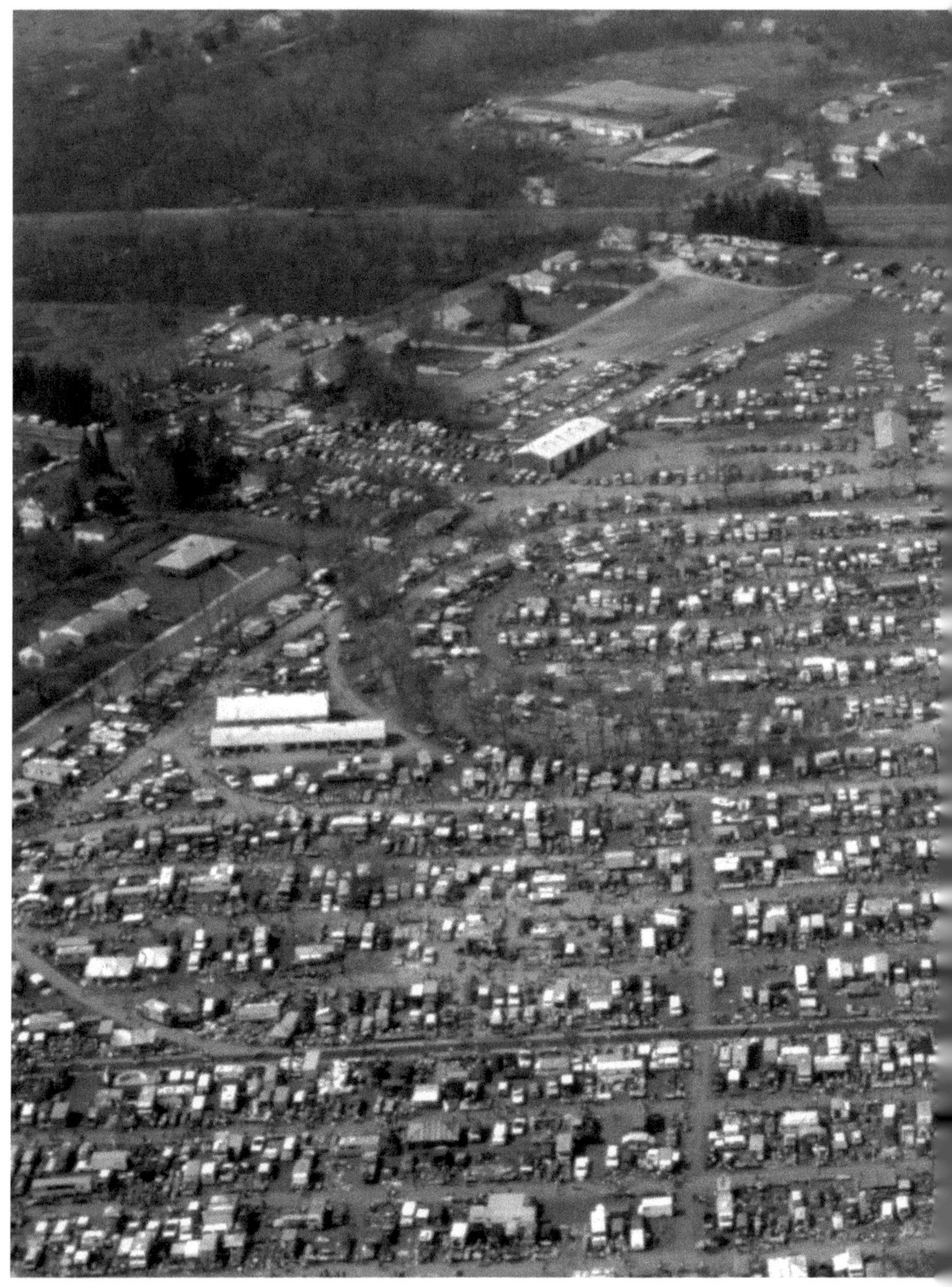

This aerial photograph of the Spring Carlisle car show was taken in April 1982. *Courtesy of CCHS.*

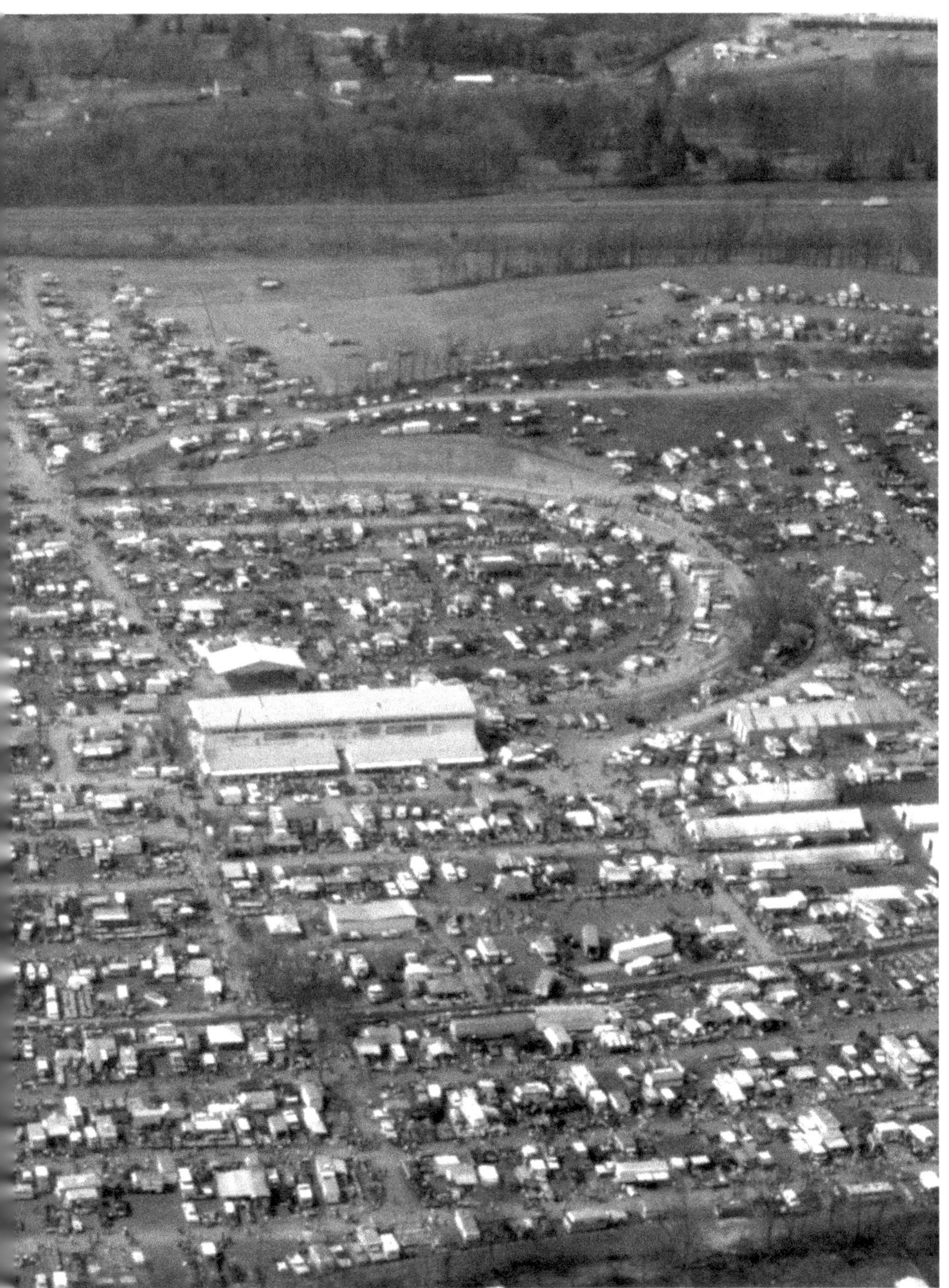

the Millers obtain the loan to buy the property. "We were two young guys with no money and good credit and somebody took a gamble on us," Bill Jr. said. "The rest is history."

From that point on, the Millers owned the fairgrounds and were able to tailor the venue specifically to car shows. They had the electrical system updated, a road network put in, a food court added and permanent bathroom facilities either built or enhanced. In 1982, the Millers added Corvettes at Carlisle because Chip was an authority on the model. As time went by, different clubs would ask them to start specialty shows geared toward specific makes or types of vehicles.

Today, Carlisle Events hosts two major swap meets and eight specialty shows, which draw tens of thousands of people from all over the world to Carlisle. What started out as two-man operation now employs twenty-eight full-time workers year-round. Chip Miller passed away in 2004 from a rare form of cancer. The annual Corvette parade down Hanover Street in Carlisle is named in his honor.

BIBLIOGRAPHY

Far West Adventures

Tousey, Thomas G. *Military History of Carlisle and Carlisle Barracks*. N.p.: Dietz Press, 1939.

Wing, Reverend Conway. *History of Cumberland County*. Philadelphia: Herald Printing Co., 1879.

"The Rum Ruins Us"

Dunehoo, George. *A History of the Cumberland Valley in Pennsylvania*. Harrisburg: Susquehanna History Association, 1930.

"The Treaty Made at Carlisle." In *Two Hundred Years in Cumberland County*. Carlisle, PA: Hamilton Library and Historical Association, 1951.

Van Doren, Carl. *Benjamin Franklin*. New York: Viking Press, 1938.

"May Heaven…Assume the Supreme"

Cress, Joseph. "Forbes Road Was Paved with Historical Irony, Scholar Says." *Sentinel*, April 17, 2008. [Article covered a "Perspective in Military History" lecture by Fred Anderson, a leading expert on the French and Indian War.]

———. "Remembering when the World's War Came to Carlisle." *Sentinel*, March 30, 2008.
James, Alfred Procter, ed. *Writings of Gen. John Forbes Relating to His Service in North America*. Menasha, WI: Collegiate Press, 1938.
Miller, Major Tad, Ret. "Cumberland County Goes to War: General Forbes' Campaign in 1758." *Cumberland County History* (Summer/Winter 2008).
Scharff, Ben. "Great Uncertainty: Pennsylvania's Defensive Measures in 1756." *Cumberland County History* (Summer/Winter 2008).

"Alone, Yet Not All Alone, Am I"

"Regina Hartman—Indian Captive," excerpted by Jack Graham, 2007. From Walton and Brumbaugh, "Pennsylvania Stories." Available online at pajack.com/stories/Pennsylvania/regina.html.
Walton, Joseph S., and Martin G. Brumbaugh. *Stories of Pennsylvania or School Readings From Pennsylvania History*. New York: American Book Company, n.d.

"Our Chain of Friendship"

Conrad, W.P. *From Terror to Freedom in the Cumberland Valley*. N.p., n.d.
Pennsylvania Gazette. "Extract of a Letter from Carlisle." February 11, 1768.
———. "A Letter from Carlisle." February 4, 1768.
———. "A Message from the Governor to the Assembly." February 4, 1768.
———. "A Message to the Governor from the Assembly." February 11, 1768.
———. "A Proclamation." January 28, 1768; and March 17, 1768.
———. "Untitled." March 3. 1768.

TURN OF THE REVOLUTION

Conrad, W.P. *From Terror to Freedom in the Cumberland Valley*. N.p., n.d.
Flower, Milton E. "A History of Cumberland County." In *Carlisle-Cumberland Book of the Centuries, The Official Publication of the Cumberland-Carlisle Bicentennial Celebration*. Edited by Albert Carriere. N.p.: 1951.

A Trade in Murder

Klenovich, Rhea S. "James Smith and the Black Boys: Rebellion on the Pennsylvania Frontier, 1763–1769." *Cumberland County History* (Summer 1991).

Nye, Wilbur. *James Smith Early Cumberland Valley Patriot*. N.p.: Cumberland County Historical Society, 1969.

Smith, Thomas Price. *James Smith Frontier Patriot*. N.p., n.d.

Tousey, Thomas G. *Military History of Carlisle and Carlisle Barracks*. N.p.: Dietz Press, 1939.

"Freeholders…Freemen"

"Our Suffering Brethren." In *Two Hundred Years in Cumberland County*. Carlisle, PA: Hamilton Library and Historical Association, 1951.

Thompson, Allen D. *The Meeting House on the Square*. Shippensburg, PA: 1984.

Wing, Conway P. *A History of the First Presbyterian Church*. Carlisle, PA: Valley Sentinel office, 1877.

"Submitted to Alarms and Jealousies"

Hoch, Paul D. *Carlisle History and Lore: Its People, Places and Stories*. Carlisle, PA: Cumberland County Historical Society, 2003.

Irwin, Roger B. *The Life and Death of Major John Andre*. N.p., n.d.

Sargent, Winthrop. *The Life and Career of Major John Andre*. Edited by William Abbott. N.p.: 1902.

Tousey, Thomas G. *Military History of Carlisle and Carlisle Barracks*. N.p.: Dietz Press, 1939.

Wing, Reverend. *Conway History of Cumberland County*. Philadelphia: Herald Printing Co., 1879.

"The Deadly Roar of Cannon with the Low, Sweet Voice"

"The Discovery of Molly Pitcher." In *Two Hundred Years in Cumberland County*. Carlisle, PA: Hamilton Library and Historical Association, 1951.

Dunehoo, George. *A History of the Cumberland Valley in Pennsylvania*. Harrisburg, PA: Susquehanna History Association, 1930.

Memorial Ceremony of 1905. Speech by congressman.

Smith, Samuel Stelle. "The Search For Molly Pitcher." *Daughters of the American Revolution Magazine* (April 1975).

Stryker, William S. *The Battle of Monmouth*. N.p.: Kennikat Press, n.d.

Thompson, D.W., and Merri Lou Schaumann. "Goodbye, Molly Pitcher." *Cumberland County History*.

Zeamer, J. "Molly McCauley Monument." *Carlisle Herald*, April 5, 1905.

GROWING PAINS

Flower, Milton E. "A History of Cumberland County." In *Carlisle-Cumberland Book of the Centuries, The Official Publication of the Cumberland-Carlisle Bicentennial Celebration*. Edited by Albert Carriere. N.p.: 1951.

Wing, Reverend Conway. *History of Cumberland County*. Philadelphia: Herald Printing Co., 1879.

"Lover of Good Order...Lament the Wound"

"Anti-Federalist Rioting." In *Two Hundred Years in Cumberland County*. Carlisle, PA: Hamilton Library and Historical Association, 1951.

Flower, Milton. "Riots Over Ratification of the Constitution." *Cumberland County History* (Winter 1987).

"Friends of the Constitution." In *Two Hundred Years in Cumberland County.* Carlisle, PA: Hamilton Library and Historical Association, 1951.

"The Sword of Justice"

Heisey, Daniel J. *A Short History of Carlisle Pennsylvania, 1751 to 1936.* Carlisle, PA: New London Press, 1997.

Hogeland, William. *The Whiskey Rebellion: George Washington, Alexander Hamilton and the Frontier Rebels Who Challenged America's Newfound Sovereignty*. N.p.: A Lisa Drew Book, n.d.

"The President Inspects the Army." In *Two Hundred Years in Cumberland County.* Carlisle, PA: Hamilton Library and Historical Association, 1951.

Tousey, Thomas G. *Military History of Carlisle and Carlisle Barracks.* N.p.: Dietz Press, 1939.

"Washington Traverses The Valley." In *Two Hundred Years in Cumberland County.* Carlisle, PA: Hamilton Library and Historical Association, 1951.

"The Work of an Incendiary"

American Volunteer. "Courthouse Fire." March 27, 1845.

Brougher, John Frederick, Jr. "Carlisle's Night of Terror." Lamberton and Hamilton Library Association prize essay, 1961.

Hays, John. "Destruction of the Court House, 1845: An Eyewitness Account." *Cumberland County History* (Summer 1997).

"My Presence…Was Purely Accidental"

Crooks, George R. *Life and Letters of the Rev. John McClintock.* New York: Nelson & Phillips, 1876.

"The McClintock Riot." In *Two Hundred Years in Cumberland County.* Carlisle, PA: Hamilton Library and Historical Association, 1951.

Slotten Martha C. "The McClintock Slave Riot of 1847." *Cumberland County History* (Summer 2000).

THE GRAY STORM TIDE

Donavin, S.K. "The Invasion: Rebel Occupancy of Carlisle, 1863." Cumberland County History (Summer 1998).

Flower, Milton E. "A History of Cumberland County." In *Carlisle-Cumberland Book of the Centuries, The Official Publication of the Cumberland-Carlisle Bicentennial Celebration.* Edited by Albert Carriere. N.p.: 1951.

"Invasion Memories." In *Two Hundred Years in Cumberland County*. Carlisle, PA: Hamilton Library and Historical Association, 1951.

Tousey, Thomas G. *Military History of Carlisle and Carlisle Barracks*. N.p.: Dietz Press, 1939.

"A Disagreeable Surprise"

"The Murray Girls Tore for Home." In *Two Hundred Years in Cumberland County*. Carlisle, PA: Hamilton Library and Historical Association, 1951.

"Our Little Difficulty"

Carlisle Daily Herald, February 28, 1896; and March 2, 1896.

Evening Sentinel. "Indian School Commencement." February 27, 1896; and February 28, 1896.

———. "A Noble Plea of Tolerance." February 29, 1896.

"Fitzhugh Lee Recalls An Incident." In Two Hundred Years in Cumberland County. Carlisle, PA: Hamilton Library and Historical Association, 1951.

ENDURING LEGACY

"A Well Cultivated Mind"

Biddle, Edward W. "The Founding and Founders of Dickinson College." Read in part before the faculty and students on Founders' Day, May 1, 1920, Carlisle.

Dunehoo, George. *A History of the Cumberland Valley in Pennsylvania*. Harrisburg, PA: Susquehanna History Association, 1930.

Evening Sentinel. "Brief History of Dickinson College." October 19, 1933.

———. "Dickinson School of Law Traces Origin to Reed Lectures in 1834." November 15, 1956.

Flower, Milton E. "History Shows School Started in 1773." *Evening Sentinel*, September 15, 1972.

Laub, Burton R. "History of the Dickinson School of Law." Read before the Cumberland County Historical Society, February 15, 1968, Carlisle.

"They…Give Themselves Up to Learning"

Black, Robert. "Pratt Brought Indian Children into Civilization." *Sentinel*, February 25, 1989.

"A Fair Chance for the Indians." In *Two Hundred Years in Cumberland County.* Carlisle, PA: Hamilton Library and Historical Association, 1951.

Hauman, William. *The Indians of Carlisle.* New York: G.P. Putnam's & Sons, 1965.

Hoch, Paul D. *Carlisle History and Lore: Its People, Places and Stories*. Carlisle, PA: Cumberland County Historical Society, 2003.

"A Young Sioux at Carlisle." In *Two Hundred Years in Cumberland County*. Carlisle: Hamilton Library and Historical Association, 1951.

"A Burst of Triumph"

Carlisle Evening Herald. "Thousands Give Welcome to Indian Athletes." August 17, 1912.

Evening Sentinel. "Olympic Reception A Gratifying Success." August 17, 1912.

Fitzpatrick, L.J., Jr. "They Remember Jim Thorpe." *Carlisle Shopper's Guide*, October 30, 1968.

Gobrecht, Wilbur. *Jim Thorpe—Carlisle Indian*. N.p.: Cumberland County Historical Society and Hamilton Library Association, 1969.

Gustkey, Earl. "Thorpe's Family Wants His Remains in Oklahoma." *Los Angeles Times*, reprinted in *Sunday Patriot-News*, July 12, 1992.

Sentinel. "Carlisle and Army Post Join Tire and Rubber in Honoring Thorpe, the Great of Greats." January 27, 1950.

———. "World Premiere of Thorpe Movie a Great Success." August 24, 1951.

Stallsmith, Shelly. "World's Greatest Athlete Put Carlisle on Map." *Sentinel*, February 25, 1989.

"And the Rest Is History"

Carlisle Events. "Our Founding Fathers—Elliott 'Chip' Miller and Bill Miller, Jr." www.carlisleevents.com.

Evening Sentinel. "Postwar '74 Events Include Auto Show." September 24, 1974.

Miller, Bill, Jr. Interview by Joseph D. Cress, June 2009.

ABOUT THE AUTHOR

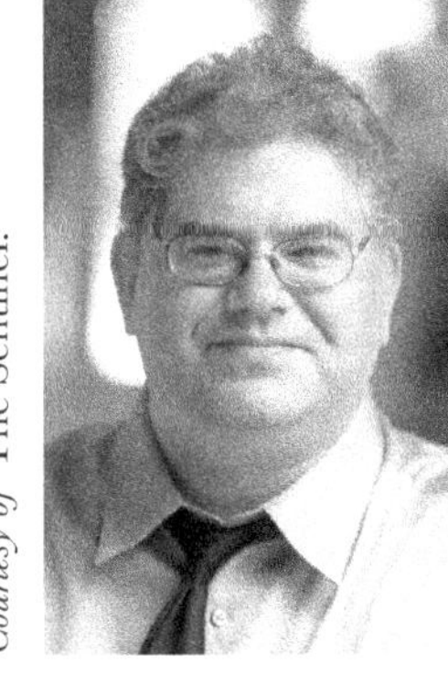
Courtesy of The Sentinel.

Joseph David Cress is an award-winning journalist with over nineteen years of full-time newspaper experience. For the past eleven years, he has worked as a staff reporter with *The Sentinel* in Carlisle, where he currently covers the borough. Cress is an aspiring author, novice poet and an amateur game designer. He lives in York, Pennsylvania, with his wife, Stacey; dogs, Dottie and Rosco; and cats, Chewie and Boone. *Remembering Carlisle* is his first book.

www.ingramcontent.com/pod-product-compliance
Lightning Source LLC
LaVergne TN
LVHW052342100826
845147LV00021B/1156

* 9 7 8 1 5 9 6 2 9 7 7 7 7 *